WE ARE SYRIANS

three generations. three dissidents.

ISBN: 978-1-60801-133-9

Book and cover design by Alex Dimeff.

Cover photograph courtesy of Naila Al-Atrash. Interior photographs courtesy of Naila Al-Atrash, Radwan Ziadeh, and Sana Mustafa.

Library of Congress Cataloging-in-Publication Data

Names: Braver, Adam, 1963-, author. | DeVeuve, Abby, 1994- author.
Title: We are Syrians : three generations, three dissidents / Adam Braver and
  Abby DeVeuve.
Description: New Orleans : UNO Press, 2017. | Novel.
Identifiers: LCCN 2017003562 | ISBN 9781608011339 (pbk.)
Subjects: LCSH: Human rights workers--Syria--Fiction. | Human
  rights--Syria--Fiction. | Syria--History--Civil War, 2011---Fiction.
Classification: LCC PS3602.R39 W4 2017 | DDC 813/.6--dc23
LC record available at https://lccn.loc.gov/2017003562

UNIVERSITY OF NEW ORLEANS PRESS
unopress.org

WE ARE SYRIANS

three generations. three dissidents.

EDITED BY ADAM BRAVER AND ABBY DEVEUVE
FOREWORD BY CATHARINE R. STIMPSON

UNIVERSITY OF NEW ORLEANS PRESS

CONTENTS

FOREWORD

CATHARINE R. STIMPSON

CHAIR, BOARD OF DIRECTORS, SCHOLARS AT RISK

As this book was being prepared for publication in early April 2017, the grossly authoritarian government of Syria discharged chemical weapons against the men, women, and children of Idlib Province. Yet again, the regime of Bashar al-Assad had violated the international ban on the use of such instruments of suffering and death. In retaliation, President Donald Trump, who promised on the campaign trail to keep Syrian refugees out of the United States, surprised the country by ordering the launch of about 60 Tomahawk missiles programmed to damage the Syrian military installation that was apparently the source of the chemical assault.

Bleed, bleed poor Syria, under your great tyranny.

We Are Syrians is an invaluable book about the resistance to tyranny. Necessary though such opposition is, it extracts its sacrifices. Telling their stories are Naila Al-Atrash, a leading theater practitioner; Radwan Ziadeh, a writer and human rights activist; and Sana Mustafa, a student. The civilization and culture of their Syria was ancient, perhaps 13,000 years old, with multi-ethnic traditions. Then, in 1963, the Ba'ath party took power. In 1970, Hafez al-Assad, a figure in that party, became president, an office he was to occupy until his death in 2000. His son, Bashar al-Assad, succeeded him and kept much of his father's administration intact. Ziadeh is critical of United States actions that gave "legitimacy" to Bashar and the first of several transfers of power from father to son within an Arab republic (p. 98).

After a brief period that promised liberalization, known as the Damascus Spring, the son reverted to his father's dictatorial rule. The three voices in *We Are Syrians* vividly document life under a modern dictator and the many methods used to maintain power for his government and himself. Some of them smack of stupidity and absurdity: Radwan Ziadeh tells of a colonel in the security services standing at attention when he receives a phone call from a general nine floors below. Sardonically risible though these incidents might seem, the methods are effective. Moreover, the Assads have their genuine supporters. One technique is the cult of personality: Children are schooled to revere the great leader and to be grateful for the security he promises. Another is to control information, within the schools and without, and censor any officially unacceptable thoughts. Still another is to conduct close monitoring and surveillance of citizens and to remind them that the government knows everything, all possible information, about them. We are omniscient, the government says, and you are not. You do not even begin to know our secrets. Because we are omniscient, and because we control force (police, military, intelligence, secret services), we are omnipotent. And, the government adds, you are impotent. A consequence is a pervasive culture of fear.

The fearless refuse to submit. At a crossroads between compliance and resistance, they feel compelled to choose the latter, difficult path. Ziadeh could have been a dentist, a prestigious profession in Syria. He gave that up to pursue his self-chosen career. Al-Atrash speaks of doing "resistance creativity," activities that recognize power and still speak truths about power that others might pick up. Courage has several wellheads. Often, a family culture has differed strongly from a fear culture. For example, Mustafa was close to an older activist sister; Al-Atrash's beloved grandfather was a legendary figure, written about in all history books, who was a leader of the Syrian Revolution against French colonialism in 1925. Her family's stature and status partially protected her. The courageous are capable of critical thinking. Al-Atrash says, "critical thinking [...] is very dangerous for an authoritarian regime. Critical thinking always opens up questions, and when you start to question, then you find out the truth about the reality" (p. 45). Psychologically, the courageous can support each other, although the surveillance society has ways of persuading friends to betray friends.

The regime has an escalating series of responses meant to silence and punish dissidents. You can be summoned to one office or another for an interrogation. Mustafa recounts the sexism in hers. These interrogations can increase in number and ferocity. "They," Al-Atrash says simply, "summoned me up for my first official interrogation" (p. 43). Passports can be confiscated. Cultural works can be barred and banned. Jobs can be abruptly cancelled. Social isolation can be imposed. The possibility of midnight raids, imprisonment, torture, and death under torture is omnipresent. Yet the regime's techniques of repression can breed greater resistance. The student, Sana Mustafa, explains after her first detention:

It was even clearer to us what we were fighting against. We'd lived it [...]. We were definitely willing to die for a free Syria [...]. There isn't any baseline of human rights. There is nothing. There is no respect at any level [...]. So when we got released we got even more involved [...]. Afterward, I was fearless. I had nothing to lose anymore (p. 136).

When jail or death comes much too near, people must get out and go into exile. All of the speakers in this book can state precisely when they knew they had to go, leaving behind their cherished country and their close-knit families. Mustafa was in the United States on a two-month State Department leadership program when she learned that her father had been "disappeared" and her mother and sisters had gone into exile in Turkey. She had one suitcase with her and no money after her fellowship was over. She could not go back to Syria. If these exiles do try and return, they will be arrested or worse. They experience constant sorrow and anxiety for their families still in Syria. How much is the regime punishing them for what the exile has done?

The myth of the romantic exile in a glamorous city is baldly that: a myth. Modern exile for Syrians can mean "extreme vetting" from the United States if they seek refugee status. Those escaping from terror are under suspicion of being terrorists. "Imagine," Ziadeh asks us, "how it feels to know your country is run by a terrorist regime and terrorist organization" (p. 118). The process of getting the right papers and documentation to cross borders is arduous. The questions of where to live and how to pay basic expenses are incessant. Forced to wander, they are the world's heroes. Despite their personal grief, they insist on suspecting the language of brute force. Instead, they speak the emancipatory languages of art, ideas, and decency.

These narrators also tell of encounters with individuals or groups that were helpful. Think of them as shelters and stations along the way. One such organization is Scholars at Risk, housed at New York University, a network of over 460 universities around the globe. Our task is to protect scholars like Al-Atrash and Ziadeh and to assist in finding positions outside of their dangerous home countries. We also act as advocates for other scholars and students who are in peril because of their ideas. Animating our work is a profound belief in the university as a center for creativity, critical thinking, academic freedom, and of service to society through the training of the next generation of competent, conscientious citizens.

Those of us who serve organizations like Scholars at Risk can do no less and must do more, given the gravity of the situation of others like Al-Atrash, or Ziadeh, or Mustafa. Authoritarian governments also seek to squelch the university. I hope that the readers of this book will listen to these three voices in exile. They bear witness to the vile wrongs of authoritarian governments and to the virtuous rightness of those who refuse to bow down to them. These three voices embody the chemistry of goodness.

INTRODUCTION
ADAM BRAVER,
BROKEN SILENCE SERIES EDITOR

How this book came to represent three different generations is, in and of itself, a product of the larger story—namely, maintaining power through a culture of fear. Simply put, initially my student and co-editor, Abby DeVeuve, and I reached out to several people who were not able to accept the risk of speaking on the record. This is not an indictment of their courage, nor is it a measure of comparison to those who eventually did agree; instead, it is the plain fact that, for some people, to speak publically meant risking the well-being of family members and loved ones still in Syria. As important as the story was, at the time some people just were not in a position to take such a risk. (And it must be noted that each and every person who declined still offered his or her assistance behind the scenes for research.) In the end, we found ourselves fortunate to have the three people in these pages tell their stories unrestricted and openly, despite the enormous risk.

As Abby and I began to schedule the interview sessions, we also found ourselves trying to make structural sense of the three very different people we would be talking with. We didn't want it to be random. It was important to us that the book have narrative connection beyond just scholars touched by the crisis in Syria.

Finally, with a little distance, we were able to see what was right before us: a near perfect cascade of generations. The trajectory of the three generations created a chronicle of experiences that spanned the nearly fifty years of Assad family rule. And beyond the individual accounts, on a larger scale, we realized that collectively the book was telling a complete story of how easily and stealthily accepted power can turn into authoritarianism.

                    *   *   *

Nothing is in a vacuum. Context shapes stories. It brings meaning to otherwise dormant parts of stories. While context may not always shine a spotlight, it does cast shadows. And at the time of these conversations there were three very long shadows: the sudden refugee migration to the West, the first ceasefire, and the Paris attacks. And while this book might not tell the political history of modern Syria, it is our hope that it tells a part of that history, as seen through some very disturbing, confusing, and frightening specific moments of time.

                    *   *   *

The first interview was with Radwan Ziadeh. Joining me and Abby was Peter Deekle, a former colleague, and a former Peace Corps volunteer who had worked in Iran. On a cold and blustery Washington, DC afternoon, we sat in a borrowed conference room in the Human Rights Watch offices. The refugee crisis was dominating the news cycle, with daily images of families floating up to shores in rafts, crowding on trains, and huddling on various European borders. The news of the past few days also had introduced suggestions of a pending Russian intervention, another storyline that was putting many humanitarian agencies on edge. But it was the nonstop footage of the refugee families—some surviving, and many not—that first and foremost overshadowed the mood of our discussion.

In terms of the chronology of this book, Radwan represents the middle generation. Born in 1976, Radwan came of age under Hafez al-Assad, the first Assad to be president. Being in a country that was shifting into an authoritarian government, Radwan found himself engaged in nonstop questioning—some practical, some ethical, and many epistemological by nature. He turned to books. To writing. To finding a like-minded community. Although he went to dental school, Radwan found himself drawn to human rights work, driven by the responsibility of the intellectual for stewardship of the future. Later, when Bashar al-Assad assumed the presidency following the death of his father, setting off the Damascus Spring, Radwan became part of the group working to write the Damascus Declaration, based on the United Nation's *Universal Declaration of Human Rights*. Threats against him grew. Eventually, Radwan snuck out of the country to go to the US as a visiting fellow, never to return. Now, from the US, Radwan continues his human rights work, both as an academic and as the founder of the Syrian Center for Political and Strategic Studies.

The four of us spoke for nearly three hours, Radwan carefully and meticulously recounting the details of his experience. Later, after the interview, when Peter, Abby, and I ate dinner, we noted that in spite of Radwan's often measured and even tone, we were struck by the unspoken sorrow that haunted everything he'd spoken about. And we too were haunted. One of us remembered Radwan going silent, shaking his head, his eyes searching along the table for an answer that would make sense of a senseless situation. And one of us remembered him saying how impossible it was that his country, with its thirteen thousand years of civilization and culture, would be run by a regime with no link to humanity. No one could have imagined, he'd said. Nobody could imagine.

In the second half of November, Abby and I went to New York to interview Naila Al-Atrash. Just days earlier, the attacks in Paris had taken place, and there were suspects still at large, and questions that remained unanswered. There'd been a heightened call from some with nationalistic views to blame entire cultures. Among others was a shared sense of anger mixed with an unimaginable feeling of grief for the loss of human lives. Needless to say, New York City was on edge, but, as can often feel reassuring, it functioned with all the energy and passion of a dynamic city, cautious but undeterred.

The night before talking with Naila, Abby and I attended a New School production of a play that Naila directed called *The Sultan's Dilemma* by Egyptian playwright Tawfiq al-Hakim. Later, Naila would describe the play by saying that in the script "the law is there, and the oppressed can resort to the law when they need it, but, when we really examine this law, we find that it was a law that was formed to serve the interests of the ruler rather than the people" (p. 64). And though Abby and I didn't know it, already we'd had our first introduction to the idea of what Naila termed *Resistance Creativity*.

In Syria, Naila's destiny may have been set well before she was born. Her grandfather, Sultan Pasha Al-Atrash, was a general and the heroic leader of the 1925 revolution to liberate Syria from French rule. To this day, he is among the legendary figures of modern Syrian history. The family tradition of service to Syria continued into the next generation through her uncles, and through her father, who served as a justice on the Supreme Court. And for Naila, even as a child, she felt the familial calling for justice for all, unable to reconcile the disparities in class that she saw around her. But while her father and grandfather engaged in more traditional paths to promote freedom and equality, Naila was drawn to the theater. She understood the power of drama, and she understood how the communal reaction of experiencing a thought-provoking concept through the stage had the potential to change minds and produce action. She went on to study and teach theater, and also directed for the Syrian National Theatre in Damascus. But as the tenor of the Syrian regime shifted and changed, it became more and more difficult for Naila to produce plays that reflected the ideas and concerns of the people. Out of that change was born the idea of Resistance Creativity—using creative expression to have the conversations that were, in many cases, being banned or being placed under severe threat. Although somewhat protected by her family name, the more Naila pushed, the more she was confronted by authority. And for reasons explained in the book, she finally was forced to flee from the country that her grandfather so valiantly helped to liberate.

We talked for hours upon hours in Think Coffee, a Greenwich Village café near NYU, where Naila was teaching. While recounting her story, Naila's emotions ranged from anger to tears to resignation. And perhaps most heartbreaking, especially in the wake of the reports of the Paris attacks, the escalating refugee crisis, and the introduction of Russian airstrikes into the Syrian conflict, was the sense of helplessness that Naila felt at being displaced in the US, sitting comfortably over coffee in a New York City café with us, while knowing and understanding what was going on with her people in her country. Some moments she questioned her own courage, and at other moments she took solace in knowing that while in the US, she still had the freedom of expression to promote understanding, to encourage young people to ask questions, and to make sure through Resistance Creativity that compassion, reason, and engagement is never lost from the conversation.

Lastly, we sat with Sana Mustafa in a classroom on West 39th Street, where, in the process of finishing her studies at Bard College, Sana was spending the semester in the college's Globalization and International Affairs Program in New York City. The first ceasefire in Syria recently had been negotiated and put into effect; everyone seemed to be holding a collective breath, not confident that it would last or even be truly honored.

While in Syria, Sana had been very active in the student movement to promote positive change in her country, but unlike Naila and Radwan, she did not end up living in the US as a direct consequence of her activities in Syria.

That Abby and I ended up including Sana in this book is testimony to just how small and interconnected the world is. After being connected to Sana through a mutual source at Scholars at

Risk, we began emailing and texting about the project, and then the logistics. Only at the very end of the planning process did we learn that this chapter of Sana's story had begun at Roger Williams University, where I teach and serve as author-in-residence through the University Library, and where Abby was a student (now an alumna). Just three years before we sat down to talk, Sana had come to a leadership program sponsored by the State Department and held on the Roger Williams University campus. It was a six-week program, and the understanding was that she and other students from the Middle East would be exposed to the systems in the US, and then be able to take their knowledge back to their home countries in order to help promote ideas of democracy. But just days into the program, Sana received a message that her activist father had been disappeared. And, shortly after, that her mother and sisters had escaped to Turkey. It was made clear that it was unsafe for Sana to return home. Thus, the end of summer 2013 began an odyssey for a young Syrian college student with one suitcase, away for a brief conference, with limited English, limited funds, and limited understanding of the bureaucracy of the country she found herself in. Suddenly she had to rebuild her life on the fly.

In terms of the timeline, it also is important to note that we spoke in the heat of the primary season for the eventual 2016 presidential election. Then-candidate Trump had discovered the traction he was getting for capitalizing on the fear and concerns about immigrants in the US. And in the wake of various terrorist attacks, such as the one in Paris, and the flow of refugees coming out of Syria, he had turned up the rhetoric about Muslims, declaring that his policy would be to ban all Muslims from coming into America. It was against this backdrop that Sana's sense of responsibility had been heightened, and was at times confusing. On the one hand, she was becoming something of an ambassador, representing the face of young Syrians in a way that might disarm assumptions and demystify the "other," but, on the other hand, she did not necessarily want such a responsibility. Still, she found herself answering the call. Despite this public role, this new calling, out of which she'd been praised and honored, there still was the reality that it was born out of the disappearance of her father and the displacement of her family (Sana herself included). Nothing came from choice. It was more as if she'd been chosen, but, arguably, in the cruelest of ways by the cruelest of hands.

And yet, as with Radwan and Naila, there is hope among the rubble of Sana's story. Hope for Syria. Hope for decency. Hope for shared values. Hope for freedom of expression. Hope for justice. Hope for art. And hope for humanity.

WE ARE SYRIANS

PART ONE:
RESISTANCE CREATIVITY
NAILA AL-ATRASH

ONE

With the theater, you have choices. A play says many things. As a director, you have a choice about which main thing you want to focus on to turn it into your main message for the audience.

How should I address these changes that are happening around me? How should I create a new language in order to talk about these changes? Because, in the first place, I considered my work in theater a kind of political and social commitment. Through theater I tried to mirror the reality. I tried to mirror the tensions, to blend the social and political concern of the people, the burning issues of the day. I've never performed or did any kind of theater that I didn't feel the urge to do. The urge of the theater is a message, and, primarily, a political message.

That's why I had a number of banned performances.

Take 1978, for example. At the National Theatre in Damascus, I did a play called *Night of the Slaves* by the Syrian playwright Mamdouh Adwan. The play spoke about Quraysh Islam, depicting how the upper class and large landlords of Quraysh (the ruling tribe in Mecca before and after Islam) used their power, influence, and economic authority to subjugate Islam at its early stages. It looked at when Quraysh was the dominant tribe in the Arabian Peninsula during the time when Islam resisted the Prophet Mohammed in the beginning. This play had spoken about when this tribe, Quraysh, decided to receive Islam, to enter Islam after a long time of resisting the religion, and how, since that time,

We Are Syrians

the tribe's members, mostly traders, upper class landlords, and wealthy people, submitted and succumbed to the religion only to serve their own political and economic interest, deviating from its path as a movement that was meant primarily to help the poor and bring justice to the oppressed.

The government knew that I was producing the play to refer to the Ba'ath Party, which also once represented itself as protector and defender of justice, only to become the exact opposite. The parallel was too striking for them to handle.

At two o'clock on the day of the opening, after I'd just passed by the theater to be sure that everything was well, I received a call from the Minister of Information. He was an old friend of my uncle's. He said, "I want you to cancel tonight's performance. I need you to say that there is no pubic opening this evening. Instead, the government is coming to see it."

I said, "Well, we can't. We've already announced an opening and people are coming."

"You'll need to come to my office now."

At his office, he showed me the list of government people who were coming to see the play that evening. Fifty-eight people. The whole government. The cabinet, the ministers. Some deputies from the Parliament. General officers. And it was all under the patronage of the first Secretary of the Ba'ath Party, Abdullah al-Ahmed.

I looked more closely at the list. "Hmm," I said. "I thought you said the *whole government*? Isn't President Assad visiting India? That doesn't seem like the *whole government*."

"If Assad were here, you know that he would plan to—but please, please don't say no."

"Okay," I said. "But I have one condition: that you won't make any decisions about the future of the play before we can discuss it."

He said, "I promise you."

That evening, the whole Syrian government came—minus one, of course. The National Theatre is on a very big boulevard in Damascus, and they blocked the three streets that led to the theater. The security apparatus posted guards at every entrance.

Everyone on the list arrived.

I sat in the front with the set designer, and with the musician and the singer who played the live music.

After the first act, I went on the stage to announce the intermission. Then I went backstage to join the actors. There was a stranger waiting in the area where we were. He said that the government wants you to get on with it; they don't have enough time for this break.

I said, "Well, if they don't have enough time, then they should go." I turned back to the actors. But then I thought about it some more. Without hesitation, I marched through the wings, not stopping until I reached the edge of the stage. From their seats, all fifty-eight of the government members just stared at me. "The break is not for you," I declared. "The break is for the actors. They need this break. Plus, the intermission is a kind of theater tradition that I love to preserve."

They were silent.

I turned my back and left the stage. And then I had the actors take a little extra time, making our government audience sit more and more before we resumed the second act.

Nearing the end of the play, I felt sure that the play would be banned. It seemed so obvious. So I asked the set designer to go to the actors and tell them that the moment they finished that they should give the curtain call. Because if the government was going to ban it, I at least wanted to force them to applaud.

And we did that.

The playwright was sitting among them while they clapped. He said that for the first thirty seconds they were stone-faced, but then they started to clap.

Of course, they banned it without allowing any discussion. The Minister of Islam, al-Waqf, which basically was an endowment for religious things, declared, "We have to hang her! We have to hang the director!" And when it was pointed out that the book of the play was on the shelves of the libraries everywhere, he said, "Yes, but how many people can read a single book at a time versus how many people can come every night to see the play?"

They understood very well about the threat of making theater.

In theater, you perform established plays. And in considering these plays, you need to visualize and understand how they can bring you closer to the people.

Are you engaging the audience? Are you giving them a kind of theater that they can be attracted to? How are you addressing them?

That *how* is very important.

What is unique about theater is that the spectators are being unified in a communal context, watching the same thing at the same time, joining into a powerful collective cry that acquires common sense about their conditions. Common awareness. A shared sensibility about their unity, and about their conditions. And that very collective experience is what encourages people to make the change in societies.

That's why the theater is dangerous.

Why dictators and authoritarian regimes fear it.

I've posed these questions to myself many, many times: How did I end up battling a system, and how did I end up battling a system through theater?

Sometimes, I might subtly change the question: *why* did I end up battling a system, and *why* did I end up battling a system through theater?

Who knows why it happened or how it started.

What I do know is that when I look back in review of my life, I think, *Oh my God. I've spent all my life just struggling and battling.*

As a child, I was inspired by the patriotic stories that took place during the great Syrian Revolution of 1925, especially those of my grandfather, Sultan Pasha Al-Atrash, the general and heroic leader of that revolution.

Every spring break and summer break we'd go from Damascus to the village where my grandfather lived. We looked forward to spending the whole time with him, hearing his wonderful stories that had no end.

He was powerful. He was commanding. But he was first of all a very democratic person. You could tell by the way he treated his wife, how he treated his children, and the way he raised the family. Everyone had a voice. So, in retrospect, it seems that during that time, my hero grandfather had been instilling something of this philosophy into our subconscious.

After the failure of the Great Revolution of 1925, my grandfather had been exiled by the French to al-Azraq, the harsh desert between Saudi Arabia and Jordan. It was there where my mother was born. In exile, they lived under a tent in a very difficult situation. Finally, the King of Jordan, Abdullah, the great-grandfather of King Hussein, intervened.

At that time, Jordan was under the British mandate, so Abdullah was able to ask the French government if my grandfather's political exile could be moved to Jordan. It was accepted, and my grandfather was able to move his family. In Jordan, my mother and my other aunts were able to go to school.

My grandfather returned to Syria in 1937, after the independence. But he refused to take part or participate in any kind of rule.

Why not? we would later ask him.

His aim, he said, had only ever been to fight the French mandate and to bring independence to the country. And when that was accomplished, he returned back to being a regular peasant living his ordinary life.

As we grew older, we realized that in fact he'd been taking a political stance. He saw how the different political figures started to share the authority between them. That disheartened him because he wasn't expecting this outcome. In 1940, this thinking coincided with the assassination of his very closest friend, Abd al-Rahman Shahbander. One of the great figures in the great Syrian Revolution, Shahbander had been a medical doctor. He was very honest, a truly sincere and decent person. Abd al-Rahman Shahbander and my grandfather had worked closely together in the revolution. His assassination saddened my grandfather so much. It led him to further recognize that there were new kinds of conflicts rising out of different political currents.

Once my grandfather came to Qurayya, a small village in the southern part of Syria, he never left. People came to him. They'd go and give their greetings. All of the presidents went to his village. For example, after the 1958 union between Syria and Egypt, when Gamal Abdel Nasser became the president of the two countries, he went to see my legendary grandfather. We were there as children, and we have pictures with him.

The slogan of the great Syrian revolution was coined by my grand-father: "Religion is for God, and homeland is for all."

Such a great, great slogan.

He'd unified the whole of Syrian under that phrase—from the very North to the very South, from East to West.

His left hand fighter in his revolution was U'gla al-Qtami, a Christian from Hauran. His right hand fighter was Sheikh Mohammad al-Ashmar, from Midan neighborhood, a tradition-ally revolutionary Sunni Muslim neighborhood in Damascus.

It was an era in Syria when Syrians were united.

And now the people who are unified against the Assad regime and this wonderful *intifada* have adopted the slogan of the Great Syrian Revolution: *al-Dein lillah, al-Watan liljami'*. "Religion is for God, and homeland is for all." As if to say that as a people, even if we don't share the same religious doctrines, we share the same land.

We are Syrians first.

TWO

How did I end up battling a system, and how did I end up battling a system through theater?

In one way or another, there always was a lot of talk about politics in our family.

We were raised with these ideals of how to speak our minds, how to fight for our principles in life, how to not compromise these principles, how to fight for justice, how to fight for freedom, and how to fight against all kinds of discrimination, of injustices, of oppression.

It seems that when you are confronted with these ideals since childhood, they are instilled somewhere inside you.

My uncle, who's the oldest son of my grandfather, Sultan Pasha Al-Atrash, was one of the first three founders of the Ba'ath Party. It was in the late 1940s and beginning of the 1950s. They were founding a revolutionary party that represented itself as a defender of the oppressed and a defender of justice (which is very ironic, considering how it turned out to be after seizing power). The Party was underground, a kind of coterie. I grew up knowing that my uncle was always being chased, always pursued by the regime. And always under threat.

Now, just for context: After the independence from France, Syria had gone through a chaotic period, a political period of different coup d'états. Between 1950 and 1953, it had known a very democratic time, with a Parliament and its various parties. But it seemed like each year we'd wake up to a new coup d'état, and with it a new regime, all military and despotic. The current political parties of the day, like the Ba'ath Party, Communist Party, and the Muslim Brotherhood, were under threat. They immediately started to hide and turn themselves into groups that worked underground.

The Atrash family is Druze, a sect of Islam from the Southern part of Syria. Druze has its own ways of worshipping and is a little different. We are a minority, just as the Alawites are minority. Sunnis are the majority, of course, but we never felt animosity between groups.

When I was growing up, we never even thought in those terms.

It saddens me so much whenever I hear people talking about Sunni fighters, Shi'a fighters, Alawite fighters.

We never thought like that. Never.

For example, when I was a girl at school, it wouldn't have occurred to me to ask my classmate who sat next to me, what is your religion? It never occurred to any of us.

Syria was always a secular country. For example, women in Syria had the same rights to work as well as a man, even before women in the United States—including the same salary range.

I grew up in that kind of country.

But that began to change in 1963, even before Hafez al-Assad came to rule, when the Ba'ath Party seized rule in Syria. Gradually you could start to feel that life around you was changing.

I was in seventh grade, not old enough to realize what was happening. But I was getting a sense of it through my father. He had studied law at the Sorbonne in France and later became a Supreme Court Justice in Damascus. During his time in France, he'd been filled with the ideals of the French Revolution—of Rousseau, of Voltaire, of *Fraternité*, *Egalité*, *Liberté*, the slogans of equality of the revolution. In my family, in our home, there was always a lot of talk about these principles of life.

Because he was a judge, he had a kind of immunity. Around the house, we always heard him critiquing the practices of the regime, particularly the secret police.

One day he came back home upset and went to talk with my mother. We overheard them, alone in their room. He was angry about someone official coming to his office at the court, and asking some questions of him.

My siblings and I heard the whole thing. We were looking at each other, wondering what was happening.

"You better lower your voice," my mother told him. "You don't want the neighbors or people on the street hearing you."

He said, "I am the judge! And I have immunity! And yet someone could come arrest me? That's wrong. It's my right to say my word!"

How I remember those words so well. They introduced the moment when we started to feel a shift.

At that time, there was an intra-party coup led by some military figures in the Ba'ath Party. The outcome was that original members of the Party were detained, among them my uncle.

One day in the kitchen, I saw my mother very busily baking crème caramel. She was wonderful at making these delicacies. But it all seemed very hush-hush. She recently had gotten permission to visit my uncle in the prison. All of the baking was being done in order to take desserts to him.

We had six members in our family. I fell somewhere in the middle: not the oldest, not the youngest. I can't explain why, but I insisted that I wanted to go with her. And to my surprise, she took me.

The place my uncle was held was like an apartment, except there were guards and guns. They sat together, my mother and my uncle, but I wasn't allowed to be with them. Of all my uncles and aunts, he was my favorite. My ideal person. The visit wasn't more than thirty minutes. I remember that I cried the whole time because I just wanted to hug him, but they wouldn't allow me to do that.

So it's moments like that when we started to feel the change. Since that time, Syria has been governed under a state of emergency law, giving sweeping power to the security apparatus. So many of our freedoms became severely curtailed, while anyone in opposition to the political regime was imprisoned and suppressed.

Ever since I was a child I hated oppression, and I had very strong feelings about issues of poverty. I was in a constant state of suffering, thinking about the poor people. Constantly, I'd ask my father why there were poor people in the world. I was maybe in first grade when I first brought this up to him, but I remember it very well. My father said, "Maybe you should live in a country like the Soviet Union." He was more liberal, like the people of France, in the vein of Albert Camus, Jean Jacques Rousseau, Sartre. So when he said that, I asked, "The Soviet Union? Why?"

"Because they have a system called socialism and communism, where you don't find poor people. People live, or should live, in economic equality."

It was as if this idea was instilled in my ear. I immediately embraced the idea of communism. By then, the Ba'ath Party had banned any other political party. But near the end of seventh grade, even though it was illegal, I decided to join the Communist Party.

I was so young to be involved with them. Twelve or thirteen. It was funny! It was ridiculous!

After school, I would go to regular weekly meetings. They took place in Nahhas quarter, in the Kurdish neighborhood of Damascus, which is on the bottom of the Qasioun Mountain. These were illegal meetings. We had to meet in secret and disguise ourselves, and before we entered the house, we had to look all around first to make sure no one was watching.

I kept my membership secret from my family. It would have put everyone at risk. Plus, I didn't know if my family would accept this idea of communism, given that the Atrash family was a wealthy family, all wrapped up in the legacy of feudalism and its well-known name.

One of my jobs was to covertly distribute the Party newspaper. They knew no one would suspect a member of the Atrash family, let alone a small, young girl. I'd sneak around and put the newspaper in the mailbox of the Ba'ath officers.

My first act of confronting oppression.

On August 9, 1967, Che Guevara was assassinated in Bolivia.

It was very shocking, and very sad news. Since the Cuban Revolution, he'd been the great symbol for us, in terms of fighting for a Marxist society. But then the Bolivian army captured and killed him.

On that same day, our cell had a meeting. I looked at the agenda, and there was not any mention of Guevara's death. The leader of our cell was an old, intellectual man. "Oh Comrade," I said to him. "I think we've forgotten to say something important that has happened in the world."

"Guevara was not a revolutionary," he replied. "He was just an *aventuriste*, out for his own adventure."

I was so shocked by that reply. I never forgot that.

In retrospect, those early experiences with the Communist Party were a wonderful time because they put me in direct contact with the Marxist theory and with other late-nineteeth century philosophies. I read a lot of Hegel, books of Engels, Marx, and others. As I grew up, next going into high school, I only started to question more and more things.

THREE

I had been to the National Theater in Syria a number of times during the 60s, when it was the golden era of the Syrian theater. I watched productions of Molière's farces. I watched Oliver Goldsmith plays, eighteenth-century British comedies. But because I was young, it never left much of an impression.

The first drama I read was in eighth grade: Bernard Shaw's *Arms and the Man*. I liked it so much—the structure, the dialogue. In high school, it was my Arabic Literature teacher who really introduced me to drama. She provided me with a number of plays: Arabic plays, Western plays, whatever. When I started to read the dramas, it just...they *burned* me from inside. I thought, I want to be there! I want just to be there, and do this! I found myself thinking, what kind of profession will allow me to do this?

Well, I knew that there was something called *directing*, but that was a far-off dream because we didn't have the study of directing in Syria.

When I was in ninth grade, my father passed away. I was traumatized by his death. He'd always been the one pushing me to be something. At first he'd wanted me to be a doctor. And then after observing my interest and passion about justice, he decided he wanted me to be a lawyer. But after he passed away, I didn't want to do either of those. The theater was one thing that kept coming back to me. Still, I was lost as to where and how should I go to college. And, to top it off, the economic state of the family was a little shaken. My father had had one of the highest salaries in Syria, and now it was stopped. I thought to myself, *Well, now it's going to be difficult to obtain this kind of money to go to university.* It was such a painful moment in my life.

When my mother found out that I was interested in theater, she encouraged me. "Okay," she said, "we will sell some land and we will provide you with the money." But after that, she developed cancer, and less than two years after my father's passing, she too had died.

The Communist Party sent me to school in Bulgaria on a scholarship. They supported me because I'd done so many things for the Party and had made so many sacrifices. There were times, especially after the passing away of my mother, when I'd lent all the family houses, apartments, and even mansions, for their meetings. They understood my commitment. And they supported it.

That was how I found myself in Sofia, Bulgaria studying theater and directing.

I started my directing studies at the Sofia Academy of Theatre Arts. It was a wonderful academy. However, very quickly I found that the life of art was too vast to just be limited to the political party you know or your own ambitions or perspectives. It is too big to put in a frame. In art, you need to see things from a much wider perspective.

In Bulgaria, the big shock was that the political reality was not at all what I'd been told about Marxism. What is *this* communism? What is *this* socialism? Once I saw it first hand, I knew the Eastern European society, at least in Bulgaria, was built on bureaucracy. Where was all this equality? Where was this justice that I'd fought for? I'd put myself all in to the Communist Party because of those great ideas. But what I witnessed in Bulgaria was very different.

I started to question many things. What was happening? Had we been told layers and layers of lies? It was a great shock.

At about that time, in 1968, there was the Battle of al-Karameh in Jordan, between the Israeli Defense Forces and the joint forces of the Palestinians Liberation Organization and the Jordanian Armed Forces. It was part of the War of Attrition. For the Palestinians, this battle was something that insured them from being submitted to the corrupted Arab countries and their regimes, especially after the Palestinian land had been stolen.

My internal questioning in Bulgaria coincided with this moment in history. It was so important, and yet there was a total ignorance about what was happening in the Arab World. And believe me, something was happening. How come we didn't discuss this here, in our party? What is our stance? What is the attitude of the Syrian Communist Party towards this?

At one point, I asked this of my comrades. "I want to know," I said, "what exactly is our position on the PLO, or the Palestinian Fatah, or any of the political groups of the Palestinians."

They said, "We are against any armed revolution."

"Okay, so then how do you see the future?"

"When the society there joins the Communist Party, their situation will get better. Then they will prevail."

Now, I'm still a Marxist, and I still resort to Marxism in many things, especially in how I understand the world and the developmental tendencies in societies and in history. But it's *very* different to be in a party. The Syrian leadership of the party in Sofia were very dogmatic. Because I kept asking questions, eventually they grouped me with some other Syrians that they saw as the troublemakers. When they froze my membership, I left the Party, taking along all of my convictions.

Some Palestinian students who were in Bulgaria had also come from the communist background. But around the time of the Battle of al-Karameh, they went to work with various Palestinian organizations. I joined them, and so it was that I met my ex-husband, the father of my son. At the same time, I began my PhD at the Sofia Academy of Theatre Arts, enjoying every moment in my profession. Still, I sensed I'd be leaving soon.

When I was still in school at the Academy of Sofia, and I'd started to distance from the Party life and into art, I began to see other things. I became very critical of the society there, in particular the communist system and socialist system in Bulgaria. It turned out that our professors in the institute also were in opposition to the system, because they were people of art; in other words, they had their own thoughts. That was a wonderful gain for us students to meet and interact with those kinds of minds. The idea of the relationship of making art as part of your politics started for us at that moment. It came directly out of that clash between the political system I was living in and the people I was in constant contact with: the professors and the wider milieu of artists.

Soon, it started to raise a new awareness about things. For me, I'd just become too disenchanted with the politics to stay in Bulgaria any longer.

Returning to Syria coincided with a period of time when many of the other theater practitioners were in a search of an identity for the Arab stage. The direct reason behind that search, as Dr. Dina Amin would suggest, is that the Arabs had been told by others and by themselves time and time again that, for a medley of reasons, theater was never born in their midst. This attitude compelled the modern Arab scholars to examine the roots of their drama in order to assess whether it had an indigenous foundation, or whether it was a wholesale Western artistic import. Later, with the help of a growing and much richer experience, I came to the conclusion that the theater acquires its identity when it succeeds by addressing people's concerns, when it meets their needs and hopes, and, most importantly, when it succeeds by inspiring critical thinking, which, in the long term, might lead to the change.

That kind of thinking has compelled us Arab theater practitioners to examine the roots of our drama. And it took us time to discover that the real identity of the theater comes when you establish a new language on the stage that can reach the people, one that will meet their needs, hopes, and concerns, no matter what kind of technique you use, be it the Western artistic resources or your traditional technique.

Back in Syria, I was among those working this through. Always asking those questions.

Are you really meeting the concerns of the people? Are you making what you are doing on the stage a shared and a mutual concern with the audience?

Because that is the identity.

In 1978, when I went back to Syria from Bulgaria, I was stopped in the airport. I was with my husband, and they detained me for four hours. It was on the grounds of having participated with fellow students and Lebanese people in a demonstration in Sofia against the 1976 Syrian invasion of Lebanon. We'd been demonstrating in front of the Syrian embassy there, and it seems they'd photographed us. You could tell, because they were asking very specific questions, like whether I was actually the one who wrote all these banners (and yes, I did design the banners). It was clear they had people spread around the world.

From that time on, I was put under the surveillance of the government.

The first real clash with the government happened that same year, when two security officers came to the institute where I'd been teaching. They were asking for one of my students. They wanted to arrest him. A few students came to me. They said there were security personnel here. I marched right up to the officials, there were two. "What do you want?" I demanded. "How could you dare be in an educational institution? You know? It's sanctity, it's sanctity! You—you should go home. Now!"

Then I dismissed them.

I probably couldn't do that now because the violence has increased so much. But at that time, they just turned and they went.

I thought that I should have been so much more scared. They'd come after one of my students accusing him of having anti-government activities. At his school.

Yet that wasn't the end. It wasn't over. After that incident, they summoned me up for my first official interrogation.

You remember the first one very well. Afterward, all the others become like a routine. But during this first official interrogation, for four hours I was put in a small room with a TV playing, switched to a channel that talked only about the Ba'ath Party, all the time showing the flag of the Ba'ath Party flapping. Slogans and slogans. The flag fluttering in the air. This went on for four hours without anyone coming in.

Finally, an officer entered the room. He introduced himself and said it was so nice to meet me. He then apologized for the long wait. "We've been so busy," he said. "There are so many things to be watching; you know, the security of the nation."

Blah, blah, blah.

"Okay," I said.

Then he started in with a whole series of empty slogans. Empty rhetoric.

After he paused, I asked, "What do you want from me?"

"Nothing," he said. "I just wanted to ask how you are. See how you are doing. Your students. See if there's anything you need."

I nodded.

"You are married to a Palestinian, right?"

When he'd asked this very innocent question, I didn't know why it mattered.

Of course, I now know why. Palestinians in Syria always were under question because at one time Hafez al-Assad had tried to submit Palestinians living in Syria to its policies, and of course most of the Palestinians resisted. Those Palestinians under the Ba'ath Party who resisted saw the harshest violence. In fact, I wonder if the number of the Palestinians that had been killed by Assad may be so much more than the number of those killed by the Israelis.

But before I could answer about my husband, he'd already moved on. "You must be thirsty," he said. "Do you want a drink?"

I shook my head. "No, thank you."

"But you must be thirsty!" And then he had tea brought in. "I want you to be comfortable."

He then asked me about my student that the officers earlier had come to arrest. He asked me about my relationship with the student. He wondered out loud why I didn't comply with the policies of the university headquarters. He reminded me that there were approved books, and that I should limit the students to only those.

I always refused that. I'd take those books and throw them out. We had a very large library in our institute of drama, and I'd make the students go in this library, make their own searches, and from there create and develop their own convictions about what they were reading. I pushed and I encouraged the students to argue, and to find their ways. But the government was very much against this kind of teaching; that is, encouraging the students to have their own minds and to create inside them critical thinking. That is very dangerous for an authoritarian regime. Critical thinking always opens questions, and when you start to question, then you find out the truth about the reality.

Following the accusation about not following university policies, the "meeting" was declared over.

After a series of interrogations, you realize that they are not interrogating you because they want information—they already know everything. Instead, they want you to be aware of their presence. They want to tell you: *We are here. We know everything about you. You are under our surveillance.*

Many people will be frightened by that. Really threatened by that. It's how the security instills fear inside you. It's how they force you into silence.

In the end, you are forced to make a choice about what you want in life. You know very well that they always are there. And so you choose. Do you want to go on? Do you want to stop? What do you want to do?

FOUR

Because my grandfather was Sultan Al-Atrash, I'd had a sense of protection. He was a figure that was read in the history books by students in every grade. Bringing harm to me was always under question. That's why, although I was interrogated numerous times, I was never imprisoned.

Believe me, there were times when they wanted to buy my silence, but I absolutely refused everything. They never wanted someone who was a minority, from a prominent family, and a public figure to gain a voice. But how could I be silent?

To an extent, as artists we begin as artists, and we are artists in the end.

The moment I went back to Syria, I began teaching in the Higher Institute of Dramatic Arts in Damascus. Later, I headed the department of acting for many years, designing the curriculums and such. There always was a way to have influence.

Still, it wasn't easy. We always were being monitored. Therefore, we tried to stage our plays in very indirect ways, getting across the ideas in subtle manners. We had to invent at all times. But oddly, that helped us. The drastic censorship pushed us to find new ways to say things, which only added to our creativity. So the censorship became something that we used for our own interest.

Editors: There are those stories of Shostakovich, about how much Stalin's authoritarianism actually forced Shostakovich to compose in ways that appeared in line with the State mandates but in fact were circumventing them. In a way, it's suggested that it may have challenged and enhanced his creative process.

Naila: Exactly! It was the same way for us. It's the same all over the world. Their tactics are absolutely the same. Such are the tactics of the intellectuals. Resistance Creativity.

In one of the later interrogations, they asked me about things that I'd said at a dinner party made up of only my closest friends. I'd invited each person. I knew them all. It seemed that the security had gotten some information from one of them, but how, I don't know. The regime has their own ways. But can you imagine?

During the interrogation, when they asked me about something that I had said, all I could think was, Oh my God. Oh my God. The only time I'd said that was at this dinner party. In my apartment!

They wanted me to doubt my friends.

They wanted to make me doubt everything.

Sometimes you'd benefit from the stupidity of the censors. Sometimes they were very stupid. They didn't understand the message, particularly when the message was artistic, and they were only looking for key words.

It became a game between us and them all the time.

Sometimes you'd think, *hmm, which is more profitable for the people: to make the message in the performance so obvious that it likely will be banned, and therefore deprive everyone else from seeing it, or to create devious ways to put things in?*

Most people in the audience would get it. They knew what they were coming to see. They knew the moment they came to a performance that was directed by me or by others with similar reputations that they would have to start searching beyond words and lines for the hidden messages.

To make change, you need to find ways to address the people. For me, I succeeded in performing my plays.

FIVE

Current events made me leave Syria. It was a chapter in a long story of opposition.

In 2000, I'd answered the call from various opposition groups in Syria to join the revival of civil society committees, what we called the Damascus Spring.

We established these new committees, charged with the aim of providing and promoting an active civil society in Syria. We tried to promote an awareness of citizenship. It was hard work. What we thought of as the terms of citizenship—civil rights, human rights—were completely absent.

However, the Damascus Spring was short-lived because it coincided with the advent of Bashar al-Assad coming to power.

In the beginning, he'd introduced himself as a representative, as a reformer. Initially, Syria had undergone a kind of liberalization. It was a very hopeful time. Hundreds of political prisoners were released. The intellectuals were given permission to speak publically in public meetings.

It was very short-lived, and the pace of change severely reversed.

Even in opposition, we continued working toward empowering a civil society. The very way the Assad regime had crashed the resistance—this wonderful peaceful resistance and peaceful uprising—by itself speaks volumes about this drastic regime. It was done all through the harshest kind of authoritarianism.

They confronted this opposition in the most merciless ways. Why? Because they realized that having a civil society's awareness among the people would enable the citizenry to meet and confront the challenges they faced from the government.

In 2001, I was dismissed from my job from the High Institute of Drama. The direct cause for the dismissal was for refusing to forcibly end a strike that took place in the institute. At that time, I'd been the head of the acting department.

The students had decided to wage a strike. Under emergency law, strikes could take you to prison, especially in the universities. The students decided to launch a demonstration as a sign of support to the Second Intifada in Palestine (because none of the corrupt Arab regimes were supporting the Palestinians).

The representative of the students came secretly to my home. It was after six o'clock. It was dark. He said they had decided to go ahead with it, even though he shouldn't be telling me about it.

Now, they knew me. I told him I supported them wholeheartedly with this. But we played a game: They knew I would have to pretend I didn't know what they were planning to do. That, I said, he needed to be clear about. And then I advised him to make sure that everyone was united under this arrangement between us, otherwise the strike will threaten everybody, especially me as a head of the department.

Next, I told him that the government is going to do a lot of things to stop this. You should not answer to anybody. Instead, do a silent strike. And that was the plan.

The following morning, I went to the institute, and the students were sitting inside the institute in a silent strike. I just passed by them and went to my office.

It hit a real nerve. The whole Syrian regime was talking about the strike. First, they sent the Minister of Culture. She talked to them and got nowhere. Then she asked me to come speak to them. I told her it's their choice, I can't say anything.

Next came very high-ranking officers from the security apparatus. They told the students things like, "you know we are with you," and, "it's Palestine!" It's blah, blah, blah, blah. But the students didn't reply. They kept to their silent strike.

Soon, the security accused me of being behind this. They demanded that I end it.

I said, "No. I'm not going to. It's their choice. Let them express their choice."

First the security apparatus had me dismissed.

Next I was banned. Banned from any opportunities for teaching or producing or being circulated in the media. Banned from leaving the country. Banned from everything except for being under house arrest.

In 2005, I joined a newly-established larger political body called the Damascus Declaration. It was a coalition of pro-democracy intellectuals. This body was aimed at asking for immediate political and administrative reforms through establishing a democratic and pluralistic way of governance.

Naturally, that was opposed in a very harsh way.

We were tracked, and we were followed. The leaders of this coalition were imprisoned. So we fractured our formal group and turned to working individually, posting petitions and articles over the internet.

Then the security apparatus disrupted our internet services and telephone services.

We were isolated by them. We didn't have the resources to communicate with anyone. They denied us any kind of connection.

Two year later, they did a mass arrest after one of our meetings in a place in the outskirts of Damascus. There had to have been spies. While I wasn't arrested, they did arrest people I knew.

This brought on a new kind of fear.

I ended up hiding in different places with three of my friends. One of them later passed away under torture. Another we still don't know about. And the third one is somewhere in the Gulf countries, but his twenty-three-year-old son was killed under torture. But at the time following the mass arrest, the three of us were hiding in a neighbor's apartment until the early hours of the morning.

I escaped, although, to be truthful, I don't know if I really did or if they just let me go. Right after that, the two others who were with me were arrested. So I don't know. Maybe my name wasn't among theirs on the security's list. Or maybe, as we say in Arabic, they counted to ten before taking action, allowing me time to escape. I just don't know.

I left Syria in 2009—snuck out of the country in a car.

Why did I decide to leave?

I was besieged. I was banned. I had no profession.

I'd visited the United States more than once as a director, mostly invited by NYU either to teach for a semester or to direct a play. One of my colleagues who knew about my situation in Syria introduced me to Scholars at Risk. That was the first time I learned about SAR. I applied to SAR's protection program that helps to find sanctuary for threatened scholars, and I was accepted. Please, I asked, find me anywhere to go outside of Syria. From the United States, I went to South Africa to teach at Cape Town University.

In June 2011, when I was in Cape Town, the events of the new revolution started up in Syria. I felt compelled to cut my ties in South Africa. For so long we'd been working to have this moment, and now that this moment was starting to happen, I was outside of the country.

It was out of the question to stay away.

I needed to be in Syria, joining my friends.

I went back as soon as I concluded the semester.

SIX

I arrived three months into the revolution.

Before I went back, I asked my family what they thought of me coming to Syria again. They were very against it, out of fear for me. At that time, Assad had tried a new series of reforms, one of which was keeping the travel ban for the intellectuals.

I was able to get someone to find out if my name was still on the list. That person was told that there were no names, apparently all the names of the intellectuals had been left off the travel ban. So I went. (Although judging by the events that ensued, they seemed to have put our names right back on the list.)

My whole family was in the Damascus airport waiting for me.

Coming through security, I was asked my name. The guard looked at me; I was trembling. When he heard my name, he said, "Who is Muntaha Al-Atrash? Muntaha Al-Atrash?"

"She's my aunt," I said.

She also happened to be a human rights activist, and was one of the most prominent Intifada, or Uprising, Syrian figures. She gave speeches in different neighborhoods of Damascus against the regime. She was seventy-something. Courageous. Wonderful. And they couldn't dare arrest her. Muntaha Al-Atrash was the daughter of my grandfather, Sultan Pasha Al-Atrash, still revered as the general commander of the Great Syrian Revolution and the spiritual figure for the Druz. It would be too risky for them.

The security guard left for a few minutes. When he came back, he said, "Would you please go to the first room and to the right?"

I went, and there I was questioned. "What are you coming back to Syria to do? Working? Teaching?"

I tried to put on an innocent face. I said, "Working. Doing theater and art."

They decided to allow me through. The guard said, "However, your passport is about to expire. So we're going take it, and you can always apply for another one."

I told them okay. For me it was very good if all they were going to do was to confiscate the passport.

Once back in Syria, the intellectuals started to search for each other. People were coming back to Syria from everywhere in the world. Once we'd joined, we started to figure out what we could do. We were working together. But it was very hard. The old civil society didn't exist anymore. It was part of a forty-year culmination of having banned people like us from holding meetings and having conversations and having dialogue. Yet still, many of us who once did the work of the civil society used our old techniques and skills to successfully organize.

We participated in some demonstrations, usually every Friday. At first, the government was very weak; they didn't know what to do. That's why they resorted to the very harsh confrontations. And gradually the uprising that started with wonderful peaceful protests for establishing democracy turned into an armed movement. With the violence, the margin for working for change started to become narrower, and narrower, and narrower.

What should we do? With the regime's control and tightened surveillance, the possibility to be active, to move among different places, and to contact different people tightened.

The slightest movement was confronted with bullets.

You felt that you were being hunted.

What would you do?

We did succeed in initiating some relief through some voluntary relief groups that provide support to displaced people, especially those coming to Damascus from other cities in Syria. The number was rapidly increasing as the violence increased. We established humanitarian relief groups to provide support to the growing number of the children whose schools were being turned into detention centers, if not being destroyed. We decided to provide these children with education. We divided ourselves into groups, in our apartments or our houses or our offices or our studios. And there, we did the teaching.

But even that was a type of activity that wasn't allowed. The regime thought it was mainly meant to benefit the people of Homs, a city that had become a symbol for resistance against the regime. The word was put out that anyone who provided these internal refugees any kind of help or support would be exposed to sanctions—from detention or interrogation to imprisonment.

Now we had a real challenge: How to keep these humanitarian teaching activities hidden from the spying eyes of the security services.

I had developed some relationship with UNICEF, so they provided us with spaces they had in one neighborhood in Damascus, which was assigned for the harassed Iraqi women that came as refugees to Damascus. There we were able to do some of the teaching under the protection of the UN.

One day, when I came back home, the doorman told me that two guys had gone up to my apartment. They'd asked about me.

I asked the doorman, "Did they actually got into my apartment?"

"I don't know," he said.

Coming down the hallway, I was afraid to go inside. I turned the handle very slowly. When I entered the apartment, I wasn't very sure if it had been searched or not. All I could tell was that there were some books that weren't in their usual places.

Two days after that, my brother's house was subjected to a terrible search. It was turned upside down. He was asked a bunch of questions about me.

Later in the evening, I posed a question to myself: Which is better, to go outside and to have a forceful or powerful voice and be under threat? Or to be inside under these suppressed voices and the pressure of the regime?

I was so scared. So scared. I wasn't young anymore. And the one thing I honestly can tell you is that I feared being in prison. I was in no way ready to be imprisoned.

That was when I started to think about fleeing again, and this time knowing it might be for good.

My son was in Canada. He'd graduated from Damascus University as a geophysicist and as a musician. He finished his PhD and was out of the country. That gave me the courage to think that maybe since he's away, I could make it, too. It was bad in Syria. We'd been hearing about people who were tortured and who were dying under the escalation of the regime.

When I decided to leave, I left via the Damascus Airport. An acquaintance with connections helped me to get a new passport through the immigration office.

I left just two months after I arrived.

At that time, for the most part, it was still a peaceful protest. No real violence yet. But the Syrian Revolution was turning into an armed conflict on account of the harsh tactics that had been adopted by the Assad regime, encouraged by the inaction from the international community. They left the Syrian rebels and the Syrian protestors at the mercy of undemocratic forces: Qatar and Saudi Arabia and whomever. Because of this, people were forced to take up arms to defend themselves.

That should not be forgiven or forgotten.

The intellectuals of that time, and I was among them, wrote letters, sent emails, and dispatched an open message to President Obama, all saying don't be misled that the downfall of the Assad regime would mean extremist groups then would thrive. On the contrary, as long as the Assad regime is in power, these extremists will flourish.

And look at the proof now. Look at the proof.

If you want really to uproot these extremists, you first need to uproot the dictatorship. You first need to uproot the authoritarianism. Because that environment breeds extremism. And these extremists, they are not Syrian. Most of them don't even speak Arabic.

Take the ones in Paris—they are coming from Tunisia, or from Egypt, or from Algeria, or Morocco. Those who have been living in Europe have grown hatred inside themselves as a reaction to the racist political regimes in Europe and in the West.

It must be admitted.

In order to fight the extremism, we have to know why the world all of a sudden has all this extremism.

Isn't it the stupid policy of Bush? When he divided the world into evil and good, when he started to nourish in the people those kinds of reactions?

I was in New York in 2003 when the decision was made to invade Baghdad. I'd been invited to a Thanksgiving dinner by my son's friends who lived and studied here as PhD students. Smart people, wonderful Syrian people. I went to their apartment with bottles of wine and cakes. I was shocked that three of these people, young wonderful smart students, did not touch the wine. And then they left the dinner. Gone. I asked, where did they go? I was told they went to the mosque to pray. I thought, but they've never been religious. I mean, we are Muslim, but we don't go to mosque. Most Syrian people don't go to mosque and pray; only the very old people do. So I was confused as to why they were doing this. Those who stayed behind told me that those students had adopted that kind of action as a reply to these stupid and racist policies of Bush, and before him, Reagan.

While I don't believe in theater's power to make change in the same *way* as I used to, I do still believe it. When we were young we thought that through theater we were going to make change very easily, and maybe even one performance could lead to explosions and revolutions. Of course that's not the case. But I believe so much that as long as what I do through theater opens up questions, then it means I am causing critical thinking. As long as my plays inspire people to ask questions, I know that it can make a change in the long term.

So yes, let's hope that I can make change through my art.

Being here in the United States, I think I can do good if I offer an informative narrative in my work about who I am as a Syrian, and what is happening in Syria. For example, I teach a class on Syrian theater and film, particularly about the controversy and politics in Syrian theater and film. I make my students see videos and films and read scripts and novels. There is a whole unit in the schedule about the uprising and the art that came out of it. Many people are surprised to learn there's been a huge amount of artwork, theater pieces, puppet theater, and movies that have emerged during this crisis. A wonderful example of Resistant Creativity.

Not long ago, a student asked me, "Naila, did you watch the Presidential Democratic Debate yesterday?"

I told him I'd watched only one part because I was busy with the rehearsal.

"I watched it," he said, "but I watched through the other eyes. I was always comparing between what we have studied and what the candidates were saying, so I was able to make up my mind about what the truth might be."

I was so happy! I was making him think and question.

When I started showing my American students the productions of resistance creativity, I discovered that most of these productions were made by my former students. I found myself talking about them in detail, because I knew them very well. How wonderful it is to see that I am an influence not only here, but also that I've inspired my former students in Syria. While reading posts and articles on social media, I'm so proud when I see their names at the forefront of such important issues.

Now I direct plays that talk about the laws and the international community. I'm furious with the international community. I'm furious with the United Nations. The United Nations was supposed to be founded and established to support people like us—to support the nations in their battles for independence and freedom and dignity. And there was something called the General Assembly, and while the larger forces obeyed this wonderful law of the General Assembly, at the same time they founded something called the Security Council with vetoes. In essence, they denied this wonderful organization, which was supposed to help the oppressed in their battles. So what's happening in Syria now, and what is happening all over the world, is it just the result of that? The UN has delayed in providing solutions to the Syrian crisis, and it doesn't matter whether Russia has blocked the resolutions or the Chinese. It is the structure of the Security Council that will always be a hindrance and will always be an obstacle to cases like ours.

Recently, I directed a play called *The Sultan's Dilemma* by the great Egyptian playwright Tawfiq al-Hakim that says exactly this. In the play, as in the "real world," the law is there, and the oppressed can resort to the law when they need it, but, when we really examine this law, we find that it was a law that was formed to serve the interests of the ruler rather than the people.

I want to talk about those kinds of issues in my productions. And I want to ask questions: Whose laws are they? What does it mean to have a law and to have democracy when the power is in the hands of the large forces?

The other morning, I was waiting in the classroom, waiting for everyone to get there. One of the students said, "How are you?"

"Good." This was three weeks after Russian strikes were targeting rebels—and not one bullet had been shot against ISIS. A moment later, I said, "You know, I'm not good. Why should I tell you that I'm good? I'm not good. I don't feel good."

Why should I say "good" by this American way of just saying *good* and *thank you*? Why should I always have to be smiling? I have my weak moments.

Instead, when this student asked me how I was, I started talking about the airstrikes and Russia and the UN and what the international community is doing about that. A foreign country is attacking rebels and backing Assad in this brazen way, and no one is doing anything. And through this, my class started a wonderful discussion. The fact that I can bring these younger generations into a level of awareness to start questioning and to start talking about what's going on is wonderful.

That's what makes me feel less burdened about why I fled, and how I left friends and family behind. In the end, it makes me feel that leaving was not so bad.

I'm still conflicted, though. I'm trying to fight back. I'm always haunted by a sense of guilt. I have two brothers and one sister still in Damascus. I worry constantly about them, about friends, and about all the people living there. Every day I read about people just passing away, passing away, passing away.

Sometimes I get this feeling when I eat something, like fruit, and I ask myself whether any one of my family members who are still in Syria—sisters, brothers, nieces, nephews—are able to eat that. Can you imagine the guilt?

Why do people take such risks? Maybe we were raised to be like that. And because it is the only behavior that we are used to, it becomes us. In my case, I couldn't do anything else. If I were a coward, or I abused my convictions or my principles in life, I would lose my self-respect, and that would mean the end of me as Naila.

I would betray my family and the legacy of my grandfather if I were not that person who fights for my principles.

Oh my God! I can't even imagine how terrible that would be.

Once, when I was interrogated by a very high ranking officer, he asked me why I signed this one particular petition: the Beirut-Damascus Declaration that said that the Syrian army should be removed from Lebanon in the wake of the 2005 assassination of the Prime Minister al-Hariri.

I said, "Well, I'm just confused."

"You, the granddaughter of Sultan Al-Atrash, who raised his family to be patriotic! How could you be confused?"

I said, "Are those demands opposing patriotic principles?"

Of course, he said no.

I said, "But maybe you interpret them in different way than we interpret them. Even the Quran, Allah's book, has been interpreted in different ways in order just to serve the interests of politics. So maybe these demands can be interpreted in different ways."

The officer asked me, "Do I understand that if you were again asked to sign this petition, that you would sign?"

"Yes," I said. "I would do it all over again." So he threw the petition in my face.

Maybe this is why I take risks. I can't do anything but that. Even when I'm confronted with the threat, thrown right in my face, I will still do something like signing that petition.

That's why I knew I'd have to leave. I know myself. I will never compromise. I will never say something opposed to what I believe. But at the time I also knew that I absolutely would've gone to jail if I'd stayed there.

There was a lot of pressure from my family. They wanted me to leave because they were very worried for my safety. They were all asking constantly if I was safe. *Are you safe? Are you safe?* They were under the burden of needing to check on me all the time, calling hundreds of times if they couldn't reach me. It didn't help that my telephone services used to be disrupted; my family always was struggling to find me. My circumstances worried them very much.

And though I still wonder if leaving was cowardly, at the time I thought a lot about my son. I thought about my age. I thought about my family. I knew that I just couldn't go to jail.

I would die in there.

Editors: Do you still feel under threat from the Syrian regime?

Naila: Yes, of course. Because the regime pays great attention to the human rights organizations.

The year after my mother passed away, I thought I should go stay with my grandfather before leaving to go study at Sofia in Bulgaria. It was the beginning of October. It was getting colder. And there in the village, in his very big mansion, I spent a whole week. I really wanted just to smell him and to be with him before going off to school.

One night we were sitting together, side-by side in one corner of his vast living room. In the other corner there was a TV. He had his arm around my shoulders. It was a little chilly and he was covering me with his *abayyeh*, his cap. We were watching something on the TV while my grandmother was preparing dinner. I was telling them about how I was going to Bulgaria to study theater, acting, and directing.

My grandfather looked at me and said, "Does this mean that are we going to see you here on TV when you're finished?"

"No not on TV, my grandpa. It's to make change."

When I think about the questions that I always posed to myself: *how did I end up battling a system*, and *how did I end up battling a system through theater*, I think about what I learned and inherited from my grandfather, Sultan Pasha Al-Atrash, the legendary general and leader of the Great Syrian Revolution.

And what does it say about the legacy of Sultan Pasha Al-Atrash for his granddaughter to have gone and studied art?

PART TWO:
THE COMMITTED INTELLECTUAL
RADWAN ZIADEH

ONE

I was born in Syria. The year was 1976.

Six years earlier, in 1970, Hafez al-Assad, the father, became the president of Syria. And then in 2000, the son, Bashar, took to power after the father. But it was the father who set the rules. The father who built the buildings of the authoritarian regime in Syria.

For more than forty-five years, we've been under the same family dynasty.

When I was six years old, my father, like many Syrian teachers, brought our family with him to the Gulf countries to teach there for much better wages. I spent almost seven years in Saudi Arabia.

We came back into Syria at the end of the 80s, just after the most troubling political crisis in Syrian history had taken place. There had been clashes between the Muslim Brotherhood and the Syrian military or security forces. More than 40,000 people were killed. And in his quest, the Assad father wiped out the city of Hama in one of the largest massacres in Syrian history.

Now, I wasn't a witness to these events. I'd been far away at the time. In fact, we had no clue what had happened in the country.

Despite this being an unprecedented crisis and tragedy, when we came back into Syria, we found that what happened was a kind of a secret history that nobody could touch.

Nobody would or could talk about it.

To this day, even the term we use to describe this period in the 80s is "The Events."

Syria is a multiple minority country, with several ethnic groups. The majority are the Sunnis, at almost 74% of the population. The Alawites are 10-12%, and the Christians are 7-8%. Also we have Druze, we have Assyrian, and others.

All of these groups lived and coexisted with each other for a long time. The culture of multi-ethnicity was a big part of what made Syria such an interesting society.

But as he sought more and more power, Assad, part of the Alawite sect, decided to make a more ethnocratic government.

After the crisis in the 80s, "The Events," the first Assad expanded his power. This move had a huge implication on the Syrian political system, especially on the army. The implications can be traced to the famous massacre that happened in Palmyra prison on June 27, 1980. There, one of the president's brothers led the Defense Brigades into Palmyra prison and opened fire on more than 700 prisoners. Despite so many people being killed, still there were some members of the army who refused to shoot. After that, Assad decided to take one hundred percent control of the security and the army, but only kept the people who were very loyal to him; and, basically, loyalty meant being his sect.

Assad then launched a huge campaign (both militarily and legislatively) against anyone that belonged to groups who opposed him. Most would be executed. This applied not only to his main rival, the Muslim Brotherhood members, but even to some Alawites who were actually opposed to his way of governing.

Thousands and thousands were executed in prison.

I remember what happened to one of the leftist political parties called the Labor Party, which was actually more of a Communist Party. All of these members were Alawite, coming from the coastal area of Syria. Members of Assad's own sect! Still, he threw more than four hundred members of this political party in jail.

And now in Syria we still pay the price of having the security and the army always controlled by one sect of the population.

In political science, we differentiate regimes: Some will consider the Assad regime as authoritarian, some as totalitarian. One of the aspects to test this definition is to look at the education system, at how the Assad regime system imposed its own ideology into all of the educational system. Not only elementary, secondary, but even higher education system.

As Assad became more and more victorious, he decided, or the political elite decided, to confer him as the immortal leader—the forever, permanent leader. As such, they amended the constitution, taking out "terms" for the presidency; in other words, he could now, constitutionally, be the leader forever.

From there, the education textbooks were revised with all these phrases about the *charismatic leader*, and things like that. Growing up in Syria, every morning of every day we had to say in Arabic, *Qa'idna ila al-abed*: "Our Leader Forever." The children. The teachers. *Our Leader Forever.* And then almost half the daily lessons had to have something to do with Assad. One lesson might be something about how we should follow our leader and exterminate our enemy. The students might ask, "What's our enemy?" Answer: "The Muslim Brotherhood's gangs."

So, authoritarian?

Totalitarian?

Either way, generations were being raised to believe it was forever.

At the end of secondary school, in my last year, there was an event that was very important in my life.

To understand the larger picture, the education system in Syria is much more like the French system, or the Arabian system. Much different than in the US. After secondary school, we have something called a "national exam." It is only offered over a certain ten-day period. And how you do on the national exam will determine much of your future. For example, if you will go to university. What you will study. If you do the best, you'll go into dentistry school or medical school, as we consider those as the cream of the cream: being a doctor or a dentist or a pharmacist. Lawyers, we don't care about them. This is the lowest in the system. But no matter what, you have to do well on the national exam.

In January 1994, the president's eldest son, Bassel al-Assad, the one who was being groomed to succeed the father, was killed in a car accident. It happened at the same time as the midterm exams in Syria.

The president decided to close all the schools.

No exams.

For forty days the country had to "express our love" to the president. It just was an enforced way to express your sadness for something you may not feel, or that doesn't really relate to you. Yes, he was killed in a car accident, but that had nothing to do with the *whole* population, which, at that time, was twenty-one million. But you had to put black flags on your balconies. No one was allowed to hear music. And those caught listening to music in their cars were detained or sent into prison.

During those forty days was the first time that I touched the fear. I saw the fear in the eyes of every Syrian. Felt it. Until then, I'd never touched the fear. Never touched it. But I touched it at that time.

One afternoon, my brothers, my cousin, and I decided just to see some kids' shows on the TV. My father and my mother suddenly closed the windows. Then they shut the blinds, blocking us from the outside.

With how Assad controlled power, we now were in the kind of environment that we called a "state of silence," or "walls of fear." If we decided to talk politics, we had to close all doors. All windows. There is a common saying in Syria that the walls have ears.

And it was that period that opened the door for me to start reading more about what was taking place. To ask why do we have to do all of that? Why do we have to live like this?

And, I believe, it opened the door to me becoming a human rights activist.

In 1994, when I was eighteen years old, I started to educate myself by reading about why we live in fear. I had conversations about it with myself, with my friends, and with my father. Before the 80s, my father had been more a nationalist. But after the crisis he decided to stay away from any kind of politics.

I began spending a lot of time in the Library of Assad, one of the largest libraries in Syria. (Everything was named for Assad. We even have schools called "Assad Schools.")

At the Library of Assad, if I needed to read any books on human rights, they had a card to order the book. One hundred percent of the books about politics or human rights were listed in red. That means *memnu'* in Arabic, which translates to "forbidden." And the list of forbidden books was long. It would have been impossible to actually order them at the Assad Library, much less read them there. So I had to buy them through the black market, which, at that time, was very active between Syria and Lebanon.

Even in law schools, there is nothing on human rights. And among the ironies is that in 1948 Syria was a founding member of the United Nations. A Lebanese man of some Syrian origin, Charles Malik, served alongside Eleanor Roosevelt to draft the Universal Declaration of Human Rights. And then two decades later, in 1969 (still before Hafez al-Assad would come into power), Syria joined the International Covenant on Civil and Political Rights.

As it turned out, all of this was just for the appearance, to claim to the rest of the world that we were party members in the human right declarations. But the point is that none of that was being implemented. And when you opened the textbooks, there was nothing about human rights.

The lesson I learned: to really understand what was happening in my country, I was going to have to read and to educate myself.

TWO

In Syria, we have only three newspapers. They are called *Tishreen*, the name of the month that the Ba'ath Party took power; and *al-Thawra*, which means the Revolution, referring to the Ba'ath revolution; and *al-Ba'ath*, the name of the Ba'ath Party.

We say three newspapers, but it's really a single edition. Because they are all the same. All share the same titles, the same information. All focus on the president and the ruling elites. They are more about personality. And, of course, always focused on Assad.

This is why intellectuals have had to rely on the newspapers coming from Lebanon. In Lebanon, they have freedom of the press, and they have very interesting newspapers. One of the most interesting newspapers that I would read was called *al-Hayat*. It has a lot of editorial opinions and engages in very rich discussions that reflect many Arab intellectuals' ideas.

If *al-Hayat*, or some other Lebanese newspaper, wants to sell their newspapers in Syria, they have to get through the censorship unit. We have three censorship units. One censorship unit is in the Ministry of Information. The other censorship unit is within the leadership of the Ba'ath Party, and the third censorship unit is within the Writers' Union.

The distribution of any daily newspaper starts at noon, because every day they have to pass all these different censorship units. And if any of the units finds something they object to, they won't necessarily ban the whole newspaper. Instead they will literally cut out the article from each and every edition.

Many days I'd pay fifteen Syrian pounds for *al-Hayat*, which was expensive in Syrian terms, considering the *Tishreen* and other Syrian newspapers were a half Syrian pound. At that time, being a student, I had to save some money. Still, I would pay out that fifteen pounds to get the newspaper, and then some days, when I'd open it, all the pages would be cut out. Nothing.

You get used to it.

In 1998, I started writing for *al-Hayat*. This was how I first came into contact with the actual agencies who make the fear among the Syrian people.

At that time in Syria, there was no internet. If you needed to send a fax, you first had to go to the Ministry of Information. They'd take a copy of the fax, send it to the censorship unit, and then the next day decide if they would send it or not. If they decided not to send it, they'd send you to the security to be interrogated about what you wrote.

In my case, I'd written an article for *al-Hayat* about the history of the Arab human rights movement and the first human rights organization having been established in 1983 in Limassol, Cyprus. The article discussed the history of why the organization had had to be based in Limassol because none of the Arab capitals allowed for Arab intellectuals to meet and establish such an organization. My piece, written in English, addressed that the very concept of human rights in the region in and of itself was a threat.

As I always did, I put it in an envelope and sent it by mail to the *al-Hayat* headquarters in London. Because of the distance and the mail, I knew it usually took two, maybe three weeks for an article to get published in the newspaper. But this one seemed to be taking a long time. More than normal. Each day I would look for my article. Nothing came out.

After one month, I received a phone call from the security.

Syria has four main security branches. Two of them are controlled by the Ministry of Interior, and two of them are controlled by the Ministry of Defense. Each one has thousands of sub-branches.

Assad made this system as a way for everyone to monitor each other. If someone missed a report, then the other one would make it. In other words, everyone reported to Assad.

All the security branches were only identified by numbers. We never knew who did what. You weren't supposed to know the function and the mandate of any of them. That was part of the control. And, of course, you never knew which people or branch might be interrogating you.

I was called to go to Security Branch 279.

I didn't learn what Branch 279 meant until five years later, when I found out it was the External Security Branch. And what did I learn about what they did? Branch 279 monitored everything written in English, following up on reports from Syrian embassies around the world.

At that time, when I'd written the article and was called in for questioning, I was a student of dentistry. Having earned top scores on my school exams, coupled with some social pressure from my dad and my mom, I decided to go into that field, even though it wasn't my first choice. In truth, I'd been very interested in philosophy. But when I suggested that, my parents said, "Radwan, philosophy? You can't go into philosophy. It's like less than a lawyer in Syria… And what does it even mean, being a philosopher? You'll have no jobs." So I went into dentistry.

Security Branch 279 first sent an officer to my university, and then to my home to request I pay them a visit.

Anybody in my situation would have felt the pressure. I was a first-time student. I didn't know what would happen or what to expect.

My parents were very anxious. They knew what had happened in the 80s. My father would always say, "We know how this regime deals with activists." He wanted me to be neutral. "It's okay to get some books from the black market," he would say, "but I have to see them before." He only was trying to help me from not getting into too much trouble.

The day before I was due to go to Branch 279, my father had spent all day contacting any people he knew who might help him find out what was going on and why I was to be interrogated. He reached out to anyone who might be able to do something to help me. It was a very difficult day for the whole family. And one that brought very few answers.

The interrogation took four hours, as they questioned me about the article I wrote for *al-Hayat*.

It caught me by surprise. It hadn't even been published. "How did you receive it?" I asked. "I put it in an enclosed envelope." The constitution says something about the security of personal correspondence and mail. How did they have it?

They said that the security is allowed to open any envelopes that have a suspicious address. And they told me that they randomly open ten percent of the mail every day, no matter if it has a suspicious address or not.

It quickly became apparent that I had very low-educated people interrogating me. Because my article had been about how the Arab human rights organization was established in 1983 in Limassol, Cyprus, somehow the officer immediately concluded that I had to have been among the eighty intellectuals who'd originally met there to establish this organization and adopt the statutes. He thought that maybe I was a very important person.

I just looked at him in disbelief. "How could it be?" I said to him. "In 1983 I was seven years old!"

But that didn't end the interrogation. How did I get these books? How did I get these words? Why am I corresponding with and writing for *al-Hayat*?

Every fifteen minutes, they put me outside of the interrogation room. There would be no water, no nothing for one hour. Then back in for another fifteen minutes, and back out for one hour. It was a game of psychological pressure. That went on from 8:00am until 5:00pm. Nearly nine hours spent for them to get their actual four hours' worth of interviews. Finally, they said, "You are okay to go, but there is no final decision. We'll let you know."

A final decision, I thought to myself. About what? And that unknown question, of course, was part of their psychological game.

That incident was the first touch between me and the security, the fear-making apparatus.

After that I became a regular guest.

In 2000, after the death of Hafez al-Assad, came a period of time we call the Damascus Spring. For six months or less, there was a pocket of opportunity while the government tried to establish the legitimacy of the new president, Bashar al-Assad. Because in Syria it is against the law for the son to succeed the father, the Assad son had no legitimacy at all. Plus, the Syrian Constitution stated that the minimum age of the president was forty. At that time, Bashar al-Assad was thirty-four.

To address these constitutional issues, the People's Assembly, also called the Parliament, met and amended the constitution in less than five minutes. They changed the article dictating the minimum age of the president from forty to thirty-four.

Knowing that this might lead to backlash from the people, the government wanted to paint the new president with a fresh look, as someone promising basic freedoms. The intellectuals and activists decided to maximize this opportunity by speaking up against the government. They issued public statements, including a famous statement signed by a group of ninety-nine leading intellectuals, calling for more freedoms, especially freedom of expression.

That changed my father's mind a little bit about my involvement, when he saw the opportunity before us.

However, we didn't have many effective tools to oppose the Assad government. We couldn't use the Syrian media. We didn't have social media. The only tool we had was the Arab media. Because we had empathy from the intellectuals in Lebanon, we published all our statements and op-eds in *al-Hayat*, where Lebanese intellectuals also published op-eds in support of us.

Al Jazeera also proved to be one of our greatest tools. When it was founded in 1996, a few years before the Damascus Spring, *Al Jazeera* was unique as a free space among Arab dominance. Before *Al Jazeera*, all the channels were run by the regimes. No Lebanese channels. No Egyptian channels. No channels of *any* country were allowed to talk about domestic issues in other countries. But *Al Jazeera* was more open to anything. Even any criticism of any regime. This was a very important step for us.

During the Damascus Spring, intellectual Syrians maintained contact with *Al Jazeera*; we appeared on *Al Jazeera*; we talked about Syrian issues. It was the only way for us to interact with the Syrian people.

However, communicating with the Syrian people did eventually get us into trouble. At the beginning, the Damascus Spring was more of a movement within the intellectual elite itself. But when it started to spread more, and it expanded its roots into the suburbs, into different cities in Syria, the Assad regime decided to interfere, shutting down all dissent and arresting everyone.

I'd published my first book in 1999, called *Human Rights in the Arab World*, through a Lebanese publisher, one of the largest in the Arab region. And, of course, the Syrian government banned the book, by decision from the Ba'ath Party. My book had no distribution within Syria at all. But that was in 1999, before Hafez al-Assad had died. In 2000, when his son ascended and the Damascus Spring began, I decided to make my words into actions. To move from being a researcher in human rights to being an activist.

For a brief time, we'd had an opportunity. All the officials criticized us, considered us enemies, called us agents of the Mossad Israel, of the CIA, and the list goes on. But we had hope. We intellectuals and activists had been using this room of opportunity to the maximum. So in 2000, along with forty lawyers and intellectuals, I helped establish the Syria's first human rights organization, called the Human Rights Association in Syria.

Every NGO in Syria has to submit its registration to the Ministry of Labor and Social Work, which we did. Of course we got the response that the Human Rights Association is a threat to national security, and thus we were not allowed. Still, we considered ourselves a legal organization, even though the government never officially recognized us. We submitted all the paperwork.

We continued to operate despite the government's refusal to recognize us. We met at the home of one of the leading human rights activists in Syria. He was seventy-nine years old, and he had spent twenty-one years in prison. Despite this, he was still active and kept an office in Damascus. Sometimes, after meetings, we would even sleep in his office if we had to.

I was on the board for the organization, and I was the chief editor of the first-ever human rights magazine, called *Tayarat* in Arabic, which translates to "Trends." Its focus was a mix of theory and discussion on the meaning of human rights and political rights. Another goal of the magazine was to bring to light the reality in Syria about political prisoners.

We eventually realized that the security was monitoring our activities and filming us. They monitored my phone and followed me everywhere. Soon after, two board members from the magazine were arrested, and I was interrogated dozens of times.

I discovered that the security was following me because all the Syrian security branches have the same car. It's a French Peugeot. We have a joke: Two security members from Syria go to France, and when they pass by the Peugeot factory, one of them says to the other: "Look at *their* security office. It's huge!"

By the time we had formed the Human Rights Association, I had graduated from dental school. But I never practiced. I got the certificate, and I gave it to my mom. Then I enrolled in more school: a program to become a dental surgeon, which would take another three years.

I used to see the white French Peugeot in front of the hospital where I was doing my surgical residency. It was during the end of the second year that I thought I might not be there for a third.

The trouble began when two members of the security came into my department at the hospital. They didn't even have a photo of me, just a drawing. They belonged to the medieval ages in their methods of security and following people.

They showed the drawing around and asked my colleagues, *do you know this guy?* Two of my colleagues warned me that they were asking about me and calling every day.

When the security reached me by phone, they politely asked me, "Can we invite you for a cup of coffee?" They had to be polite because at that time intellectuals and activists felt empowered. We had the media focused on our cases; we could do whatever we wanted, fear-free, for a short time.

It was requested that I come to the Security Branch 291. Of course, I didn't know what Branch 291 meant. Later on, I discovered 291 was part of the Military Intelligence branch of Security.

But I'm not a military guy. Why did I have to go there?

The Deputy Director of Military Intelligence was Assef Shawkat, who also happened to be the brother-in-law of the President, Bashar al-Assad. Shawkat was the Number One in charge in Syria. At the time, it was very rare to have a conversation between you and the head of the security. But Shawkat, also known as the Major General, personally invited me into his office to have a "conversation."

The building had nine floors. First, they took me up to the ninth floor, where I sat waiting with a colonel.

Finally, the phone rang. It was Shawkat, whose office was on the ground floor. And when the colonel answered, he stood up. While on the phone! Imagine: on the phone the colonel has to stand up when he receives a call from the Major General nine floors below. This is the way of fear. The colonel didn't know who might be watching. Maybe someone who handles the coffee in his office? He didn't know who might report whether or not he showed the proper respect for his superior. Even nine floors up. By phone.

I was taken downstairs to meet with Shawkat. About four hours into the "conversation," he made me an offer to work as a consultant for Bashar al-Assad.

I received the message he was sending. Still, I refused to work or to write anything for him; I rejected him in a polite way. I understood the way of fear.

He thanked me for coming.

The next day, just at the end of the second year of my surgical training, the security had me dismissed. Fired. For "national security" reasons.

The troubles had really started.

Some of my friends were supportive. Some even asked me to have regular meetings with them to exchange ideas. But after the crackdown on the Arab Spring, everyone was afraid. They even deleted my name from their cell phone contacts. Later on, when there was Facebook, some of my "friends" on Facebook eventually removed me from their friends list. The fear reached us even there.

THREE

The Ba'ath Party took power in 1963. When Hafez al-Assad assumed control in 1970, the Minister of Foreign Affairs came with him, and the Minister of the Interior came with him, and so on and so on and so on. The Minister of Defense, Mustafa Tlass, stayed in his post for more than thirty years. Or take Najah al-Attar, the Minister of Culture (although they recently upgraded her into Vice President for Culture Issues): she basically is in the same post today that she's been in since the 70s. There was no new blood in the political positions, and that only expanded into intellectual life, political life, and cultural life. They were all frozen.

The intellectuals who decided to speak up in 2000 were mixed. There was no "circle of elites." Instead, it was a mix of new generations, people like me, who were newcomers inspired by new ideas and universal values like democratization and human rights. You also saw some intellectuals who grew up outside of Syria—in France, or elsewhere in Europe—and had come back into Syria and then decided to join the movement.

The elite. The political parties. The communist parties. None of them had any role in the era of the Damascus Spring.

No, it was all of us who grew up on the idea of the responsibility of the intellectual, or what's called the Committed Intellectual. You have to be committed to your social responsibility, to the destiny of your nation. Or to use the quote from Marx: "The point is not merely to understand the world, but to change it." We did not learn this in school—all of us grew up with the notion that intellectuals feel they have more responsibility than others.

Riad Seif, a former member of Parliament, was interested in some of the ideas from the Forum for National Dialogue, a human rights organization that played a key role in the Damascus Spring. Riad Seif was not actually a political activist. He had no such background. He was a businessman whose factory produced Adidas for the whole Middle East market. He was a very successful guy. More than fourteen hundred employees. His success with Adidas branded him as the new model of the Middle Eastern businessman. But Seif got inspired by the ideas of change. In 1999, during Hafez al-Assad, he felt that as a member of the Parliament he had some responsibility. All members of the Parliament in Syria we call "Rubbers"—Rubber Stampers. In general, they had nothing to do, having only been appointed by the security. But Riad Seif belonged to the Damaseen family, a very aristocratic family in Damascus, and he felt a sense responsibility. Plus, he had money.

Riad Seif and I became friends. We spent a whole night together writing about the issues, and then planning. We decided to open the new house he'd bought for a forum. The first lecture would be about the civil society, and the role of the civil society. We invited Antoin Makdesi, a Syrian Christian philosopher who has great respect among the Syrian intellectuals. Makdesi had translated all the books from French into Arabic, German to Arabic. At that first forum, he spoke about the civil society. The second forum, held in February 2001, featuring a presentation by Yousif Salamah, was more about the constitution and democratic change.

The subsequent forums had discussion and lectures that were more general—the nature of civil society, the role of the constitution in general. But I wanted to maintain the focus on democratic change in Syria, and why the ruling party never changed, and how we had to challenge the ruling party. It was very strong talk.

And there, taking place at that house, those forums really were the beginning of the Damascus Spring.

But then the Assad government decided to stop all the forums in all the private houses.

Editors: Do you think those were being monitored?

Radwan: Of course. Everything.

The security sent us a warrant to close the forums. Not to do it again. But we decided to open the forums again. After we did an interview with *Al Jazeera*, the security came and arrested Riad Seif himself. They took away his immunity from being a member of parliament, and they put him in prison. Also they arrested some of my friends.

Al Jazeera was covering that daily. Everyone talked about it in the newspapers—the end of the Damascus Spring. By that point, I was being interrogated nearly every single day.

I always had my bags packed to go to prison. On any given day they could come at 4:00am and take you to prison. You had to prepare yourself.

In my case, the interrogations were more verbal. But others I presumed probably had some physical interrogation. The security officers would tell me this was the end of the Damascus Spring, that it wasn't allowed by the government.

Despite the regular interrogations and threats, we still believed we had much of the world on our side. But then came 9/11. And all the media attention shifted to the United States. We paid the price of being victims of inattention of the media. Because every channel's focus, including *Al Jazeera*, was on the huge event in the Unites States. The Syrian government knew it could do whatever it wanted without worrying about bad publicity.

We lost the battle. The media battle at least. Nobody was watching us.

Ironically, the Assad regime offered its assistance to the United States, as all dictators do. And soon Syria found itself in the middle of the global war on terror.

In June of 2000, Madeleine Albright, the US Secretary of State at that time, came to Syria to attend the funeral of Hafez al-Assad. Hafez al-Assad had had a good relationship with President Clinton. In fact, they'd met three times regarding the peace negotiations with Israel. While in Syria, Albright met with Bashar al-Assad for fifteen minutes. In a press conference when she left Syria, the Secretary said how sorry she was for the loss, and she added, "the transition is very smooth."

We all point to that moment as the one that that gave Bashar al-Assad legitimacy. International legitimacy. It was a signal that nobody was allowed to challenge the transition from the father to the son.

It was the first such transition from father to son within a republic, which then encouraged other countries to do the same. In Egypt, Mubarak started to prepare his son Jamal; in Yemen, Ali Abdullah Salah prepared his son Ahmen; in Libya, the leader prepared his son, Saif al-Islam, to succeed.

Secretary of State Madeline Albright's statement was run in all the newspapers in Syria. I still remember it: "The transition is smooth."

Stability.

That was the debate at that time, to consider the stability in Syria.

So the US supported "continuity" and "stability" rather than having a democratic transition. That's around when George Bush came into power, and still the relationship between Syria and the US remained the same.

But with the Iraq War, the relationship started to change, and the US embassy closed. The Assad regime stood against the Iraq War, and started to send some jihadists into Iraq to make trouble for the United States because the Assad regime thought that if Iraq gained some stability, then the US troops would move into Syria.

Editors: And yet after 9/11 Assad is saying, "I'll help you any way I can" to the US?

Radwan: Yes, and for us, all the intellectuals and activists, everyone was waiting, wondering when we would be arrested or detained. While we continued to meet in secret, we were careful not to give interviews, public statements, etc.

Editors: You said that it seemed like everyone around you was getting arrested, your friends too. How did you avoid getting arrested, and why do you think they didn't come get you in the night?

Radwan: I've been asked this question many times. It's very difficult to answer. It's something that seemed to happen randomly. You didn't know why exactly this person was detained and not that person. Some of the people who were detained, two of them that at least come to mind, had very, very low profiles. Some of them had a higher profile like me, and others had never been detained; for example, the lawyer who was the head of the Syrian Human Rights Association has never been detained or arrested. Nobody knows how the security decides.

We took some steps to protect ourselves. If we needed to sit for a conversation, we had to turn on the TV and put on the channel with the static and white noise. We had old phones, Nokia and others, so we would take the batteries out. But these were stupid steps—the security always had microphones in the rooms. Basically, they got everything.

So many people were detained. Some were arrested based on secret conversations being monitored. Others because they did interviews for *Al Jazeera* and other outlets. But I got a different prize. They withdrew my passport. I was banned from traveling. This directive came from not only one security branch, but from three different security branches. They fired me from my hospital and banned me from any further studies.

During this time, the security regularly threatened my family, especially my father and sisters. They told my father, "you have to stop your son's activities." My mother was very scared and concerned about what would happen.

It was a serious issue.

But we continued in private ways. No money. No public statements. Nothing until 2003. That year, the Iraq invasion gave us intellectuals some room. The Bush Administration put on their freedom agenda. I know it's debatable here in the US whether the Bush Administration was sincere about this, but even when they didn't discover weapons of mass destruction in the region, the Bush Administration did discover a lack of freedom there. And that became the so-called freedom agenda.

Every day, Syria was under pressure from statements by Bush, implying that maybe Syria would be next after Iraq. As intellectuals we decided to use the room at that time. We stood up and we issued public statements about the need for national reconciliation. If Syria was really under threat, as the regime said, then we couldn't resist the American pressure if there was no national reconciliation. Of course, the Assad government threw our statements in the trash and arrested some people who signed the statements.

The public space we knew had been closed; the government wouldn't accept any kind of criticism.

Every Syrian has to serve in the military, but because I was a student, then a doctor, I had been able to postpone it. But you can't postpone it forever. You have to do it. The security used this as an excuse to send police into my home on a regular basis. So I decided to sleep in different apartments. For six or seven months I was hiding. But I had no passport to travel; I couldn't live in hiding forever.

Finally, I decided I should go to the military. I spent two years there, sent into the desert. They were the worst years in my life.

But at the same time, it was a good opportunity for me to get to know the security and the army from the inside. To learn how they were thinking and how they lived. It was also a good opportunity for me to continue my reading. I read hundreds and hundreds of books in those two years. I had nothing to do—read books, read books, read books.

It was very difficult, but in 2005, when I finished my military service, I asked to get my passport back and to have my travel ban lifted. This request reignited them to interrogate me. Again, and again, and again. After seven months, they decided to give me back the passport. Why? Because in light of a bad relationship with the US, the Syrian regime was under pressure to have a good relationship with the European Union.

In 1996, the EU had made a new policy called the Barcelona Declaration, meant to encourage the relationships between the EU members and the countries surrounded by the EU in the north and south. Since Syria has access to the Mediterranean Sea, it could be part of this process, not as a full member, but as one who could benefit from trading with all EU members.

However, in Article 2 of the Barcelona Declaration, it states that its associate members should respect and implement human rights. So, as a way to answer to some of the pressure that the Europeans put on Syria concerning its human rights record, the Assad regime took small steps to say things like, "Oh, I allowed Radwan Ziadeh to travel, and others were released from prison." In fact, in 2005 they released all of the prisoners of the Damascus Spring. They even suspended some others' whole prison terms.

Once I was handed my passport, I took my first trip into the United States.

While in the US, I gave a lecture about the human rights situation in Syria. But the Syrian ambassador attended the lecture, and then he reported me!

When I returned to Syria, I got a phone call the very same day I got back. The entire interrogation was about my talk in the US.

They decided to put me on a travel ban again. They took away my passport for another year.

That was 2006.

My friends and I created something called the Damascus Declaration for Democratic Change. We'd started thinking we should put all the opposition together under one umbrella. Now some of these "political parties" that we proposed for our coalition maybe only had three or four actual members. We needed everyone. Even though we knew these individual political parties had no weight, taken all together they could mean something.

We had a conversation with one of the communist parties, and it took a week for them to accept and sign the declaration. The leftists and the Communists used to argue on every word (*What's its meaning, capitalism? Why do we have social democracy? We have to put something about social rights*). It was difficult, but it was a good exercise. When you build a coalition in any democratic change it's difficult, especially to put the right and the left in the same coalition.

We ended up with the Damascus Declaration, which was only one page. I'd written the first draft.

The final version, after nine months of negotiations, ended up much different than the initial draft.

But by the end, we'd been able to have an umbrella that could put groups like the Muslim Brotherhood alongside with the Communists—something that was a huge achievement if you consider the struggles to make broad coalitions during similar-minded transitions in Eastern Europe, especially, for example, in the Czech Republic.

The Assad government responded by imprisoning all forty members of the leadership of the Damascus Declaration.

I narrowly escaped being arrested during that sweep. At the time, the Intelligence had granted me a one-time permission to go into Lebanon, which I then used to travel from Lebanon into Spain for a conference. So I'd been away when the detainments happened.

But when I returned, it was clear that the space had become more and more closed in.

The final push that made me decide to leave the country followed a book I'd published in Egypt in 2007 called *Decision Making Process in Syria*. It was about the structure of the Assad government and how its foreign policy decisions were made. Of course, all my books were banned in Syria, this one included. But soon after the book was out, I received a phone call from the head of the security at that time "inviting" me for a talk. When we met, he started interrogating me about what I'd written. He was very angry because in the book I'd mentioned that the former president, Hafez al-Assad, knew that the election was a joke, and that basically it had been a lie to continue the election.

The head of security said to me, "You are calling him a liar, yeah?"

"I did not say that."

It went on and on. At the end of the interrogation, he said, "So you know, this is the last time you will visit us as a guest."

The message was clear: the next time I was called, I would be put in prison.

After that happened, I realized I had nothing left to do inside Syria. I had actually received a fellowship with the United States Institute of Peace (USIP), but I kept postponing it because I felt that I had to stay in Syria, that I had something to do in Syria. I knew if I went, I wouldn't be able to come back.

I'd just gotten married when we discovered my father had an advanced stage colon cancer. That was a very, very emotional thing. We didn't have the treatment for it in Syria; I would have to go into Jordan to get the medicine. Yet I still had the travel ban.

At this time, the Assad government, along with the European Union, were in the final stage in the negotiation about the formal association between the two governments, in relationship to the Barcelona Declaration. A high level delegation came from Europe to visit Damascus. They met with me for dinner before they met with the Minister of Foreign Affairs. I told them my story, explaining that I'd have to go into Jordan to find the medicine for my father.

On my behalf, they talked to the Minister of Foreign Affairs, and the Minister of Foreign Affairs talked to the security. Security refused any accommodations the first time. After a second discussion, I actually got permission to travel.

I knew that if I went, then maybe this would be the last time.

Even though my father was sick, he told me, "Radwan, go and accept the fellowship with the USIP." He told me not to bother with his medicine, and that I should use this chance to get to the United States.

After a long debate with my father and my mother, my wife and I decided what to do.

We told the security we were going into Jordan for the medicine. Then we spent one night in Jordan, and from Jordan we flew toward the US.

When I was in the Lufthansa from Amman into Frankfurt, Germany, then from Frankfurt into Washington, DC, I remembered the similar trip that the great Syrian thinker Rashid Rida made in 1907, exactly one hundred years before me. He'd decided to leave Syria, at that time under the Ottoman Empire, because there was no space for freedom in Syria at that time. Rashid Rida first went to Egypt, and from Egypt into Paris—which, along with London, was the capital of knowledge at that time. As I made my trip, I remembered the writings of Rashid Rida. I thought about how I'm going now on the same trip into the West. Going off to the capital of knowledge, which in my time is the United States.

This was the 29th of August, 2007.

The day I left Syria and didn't go back.

My wife and I still often discuss our choice to leave Syria. She is a physician. She is not involved in what I do. My wife sees me taking these risks, and she would like me to stay away from them, especially now that we have three children. Three boys. She likes to keep them away from my work because she knows what could happen, especially when everyone sees what's going on in Syria right now. She wants to at least raise the kids away from that.

When I left Syria, I put all my family members at risk. My mother, brother, and sisters all paid the price when the Syrian government discovered I was in the US instead of Jordan where I told them I was traveling. The week after I came to the US, I appeared on CNN and talked about Syria. In response, the security branch put a travel ban on all my family members. Mother, brother, sisters.

The difficult part was my sister's story. She has six children and lives in Syria, but her husband is working in Saudi Arabia. When they gave them a travel ban, he couldn't get in, and she couldn't get out. She's gone through tremendous effort to try to travel, but every time she went to the security they said *no* because of my activities. Sometime they show her tapes or videos of the interviews I did.

She's been in this situation almost since I've been gone. It's very difficult for her.

And I know I'm responsible.

They put out a warrant for my arrest if I ever returned.
   My father died in 2009. I couldn't attend his funeral.

FOUR

When we arrived in the US in 2007, my wife and I went to a hotel. We spent a few nights there before we started renting a house. I was a little bit familiar with the US system because I had been here on two visits before.

I was in the US under a J1 visa, for a professor exchange. It could be extended up to five years. I never applied to get a green card because I was thinking I would go back into Syria at any opportunity. But after the Syrian uprising and the trouble in the country, the United States Congress gave temporary protected status, or TPS, to the Syrian citizens who were living here.

I am still living here under TPS as we speak.

My first year in the US was spent with the USIP. A year later, I wrote my first book published in English, *Power and Policy in Syria*. I also started connecting with Scholars at Risk, who referred me to Harvard University. I spent the second and third year as a Scholar at Risk at Harvard University at the Kennedy School of Government's Carr Center for Human Rights Policy

Over the years, I moved from university to university: Harvard, NYU, Columbia University, George Washington, Georgetown. Thanks to Scholars at Risk, and to the Scholar Rescue Fund, I spent time in very good universities. And in each city, I started to engage with human rights organizations such as Human Rights Watch, Amnesty International, and think tanks in Washington, DC.

It was a huge opportunity to connect with the US intellectuals—it opened new doors for me of knowledge and experience that I never dreamed were possible when I was in Syria. And this was thanks to Scholars at Risk and Scholar Rescue Fund; those two leading organizations were able to see that someone who was supposed to be in a prison in Syria instead was making his way to Harvard.

But when I first arrived, nobody cared about Syria. Nothing compared to Egypt or other Arab countries that, at the time, had been the subject of tremendous books and interest. This is why, along with a number of Syrian scholars and friends like Osma Kadi, in 2008 I established the Syrian Center for Political and Strategic Studies, of which I am still the director. I wanted an organization to raise awareness about Syria.

To get started, we decided to bring in some people to serve on the board—mostly the few professors and teachers with knowledge about Syria.

I think I filled a gap at that time. It was very useful for me. Having the Syrian Center for Political and Strategic Studies allowed me a place to try to influence decision-making about Syria from here, as well as giving me opportunities to connect with others.

When you are living in a closed society, like I was, knowledge is very limited. But when you are in the US, you turn one hundred and eighty degrees. Different experiences and knowledge in other regions in the world are opened up to you. I became interested in the transition to a democratic system in Eastern Europe, and in the similar transition and justice in Latin America. I traveled to both of those places, which had a huge impact on my study and my research.

After the uprising of the Arab Spring started in March 2011, I was active from day one, doing what I could from outside Syria. We saw it as an opportunity to rebuild Syria again, to participate and to lead in the democratic transition. No one anticipated that we would have this chance. I spoke out against the human rights violations, what was happening in the country, and, of course, the Assad government. I became very high profile, showing up in the media every day.

That was, and still is, very difficult for my family members. Especially my mother. Following the 2011 uprising, my mother decided to go into hiding. Every day she would hide in a different place.

I was born in a city called Darayya, seven kilometers outside of the heart of Damascus. It's where we lived. In August 2012, the worst massacre in the Syrian Revolution up to that point happened when the Assad security forces came into my home city and slaughtered 713 civilians. It became known as the Darayya Massacre. Among the casualties was one of my cousins. Between the actions of the Assad regime and the inaction of the US, Syria ended up undergoing the worst humanitarian crisis in its history.

My mother and brother were still inside Syria when this happened. I told them, "you have to get out." And so they took the risk of actually driving from the suburbs of Damascus to the north into Turkey.

The armed conflict was going on; it was very dangerous for them to make this trip. We actually organized the journey along with the Free Syrian Army, an armed opposition. They knew me from seeing me on TV. My mother and brother spent three days making this trip. They arrived safely into Turkey, but without any documents—no IDs, no passports, nothing. In Syria, they hadn't been allowed to get a passport because of their travel ban from the security.

And to this day, as are many refugees from Syria, they are living in Turkey without any documents; the Assad government will not grant them any passports to travel.

As we talk, I've been in the US for nine years now. I love this country.

You can't actually know the United States if you just live in Washington, DC. I've visited all fifty states. I wanted to know more about the history of this amazing country and the people here. Each different state, I discovered, has a different personality and a different history. All of them have contributed to the greatness of this country.

Even here in the US, I still feel under threat. I feel it, but it is not something that concerns me every day. Of course, I regularly get threatening Facebook messages. Sometimes phone calls. There have also been many incidents. For instance, we organized a conference in 2013 at Lehigh University, where I was a visiting scholar on Syria. Almost seventy Assad supporters came with slogans against me, making direct threats that didn't stop until the police came and dispersed the crowd.

You lose a sense of connection and community when you come to a new culture. There is no such kind of social life. My wife feels it a lot. I might feel it less because I'm very busy with my work and I travel often. But my wife, she always talks about it. She especially misses her family. Sometimes I feel it, but not like my wife does. And always I say to my wife, "this is the balance." To get the knowledge, the best education, you have to lose something.

That's also reflected in my theory about the relationship, or perhaps contradiction, between economic growth and social life. The first thing a kid does here in the US when he grows up is to look for opportunity rather than to stay with his father or with the family. *Work, work, work,* they say. In Syria, or in the whole Middle East, we prefer to stay with the family, in part because there are not many opportunities. If there is economic growth— any increase, or any change—that will reflect on the social life. I mean, if I'd found much more opportunity in Aleppo, the second largest city in Syria, I would've gone there. But because there are no such opportunities, everyone prefers to stay with family.

Editors: You've taken tremendous risks since you were eighteen. Do you wonder sometimes, why me? Do you feel you were chosen to do that?

Radwan: I'm not chosen. I grew up with making hard decisions and taking responsibility for my decisions. Of course, sometimes I make stupid decisions, but I feel like I'm blessed because they always seem to end up having been the right decisions—even when some decisions had huge implications, or even though some people wouldn't have made the decisions I did. Like the decision to leave dentistry to go into political science. Or the decision to leave Syria to go to the United States. Of course, all of these decisions bring some implications for your family life and your personal life. And I take it. I take it with the full responsibility. My wife embraces that about me, and sometimes we have discussions about these hard decisions.

Editors: You're clearly still dedicated to the same things you were twenty years ago.

Radwan: 24/7.

When the 2011 uprising started, the hope was that we would have a smooth transition into a democratic system. I hoped to contribute all my knowledge about how Latin America and Eastern Europe did the transition through negotiation and peaceful means. I hoped to see Syria as a democratic country. I got a lot of attention from the Syrian public, and I'm now well known for my ideas. I can say I have some respect, especially among the intellectuals, for approaching the solutions differently than other ideological oppositions by having a more academic background, one that allows me to refer to some of the lessons we can learn from other countries. For me, that is important.

But we also believed that the US should do something about Syria from the beginning. The US should not leave this authoritarian regime to do whatever it believes, to kill its own people, gas its own people, and now use indiscriminate bombing, especially the barrel bombs.

I have been seen as interventionist for asking for intervention from the US into Syria.

Look at the mess in Syria. If we'd had US intervention early on, we would have saved the lives of thousands and thousands of people, among them maybe my cousin who'd been killed in the Darayya Massacre.

But Syria turned into armed conflict. In any armed conflict, any human, or even human rights organizations, always ends up immobilized. The language of arms is stronger than the language of ideas (which this is the only language I have). Nobody will buy the ideas if you don't have the power or the authority to implement them on the ground.

That's what led Syria into the worst humanitarian crisis.

These are the worst days of our lives.

We spend a lot of moments crying when we see the videos of Syria on YouTube every day. For example, when the Russians began bombing the Syrian civilians in 2015, it was like witnessing a loss of hope. The Syrian people can't fight every power in the world. Iranians. Hezbollah. The Assad government. The Russians. It's too much.

And then, of course, there is ISIS. Recently, they put fifty-six names on their "hit list." And they put me first to be executed if I go inside Syria.

Imagine how it feels to know your country is run by a terrorist regime and terrorist organization—the *worst* terrorist regime and the *worst* terrorist organization.

Editors: Is it worse than you imagined?

Radwan: Worse. Worse by far. Worse by far. Nobody anticipated or imagined that this country with thirteen thousand years of civilization and culture—with Damascus, the oldest inhabited city in the world, for its capital—would be governed by a mass killer and an organization with no link to humanity, like ISIS. Nobody could imagine.

Editors: Do you see in your lifetime a Syria that you will return to?

Radwan: I hope so. And I still work for that.

My son has actually always acted like a US citizen. Even though we have Arabic channels and Arabic TV, he can't understand Arabic as well as his parents. I don't know how he got English and no Arabic. We even enrolled him on Saturdays and Sundays in Arabic school, but he still speaks English much better than us. We needed him to get the best of the education system.

But when anyone asks: "Where are you from?" He responds, "I'm from Syria," even though he doesn't know where Syria is on a map.

He only knows the Syria we remember. We never open images or videos of the current Syria in front of the family members. We don't want him to grow up knowing such violence.

For him, Syria means delicious food.

PART THREE
WHEN THE REVOLUTION STARTED:
SANA MUSTAFA

ONE

It was early September 2011, around 12:30am. I was nineteen, living in Damascus and working toward my undergrad degree. My older sister Wafa was out participating in a demonstration. They took place all the time, often going late into the night and early morning.

Wafa is an outstanding activist. She was one of the first to be in the streets in Damascus, forming groups and organizing demonstrations and protests with other college students. I was involved, but not nearly as much as she was.

That early September night, Wafa, still at a demonstration, received a call from a friend of ours saying, "I want to meet you now." At the demonstration she'd bumped into my cousin Amr, also an activist. Together, they went to meet her friend. But it turned out he'd been captured. He'd been made to call and tell her to come. A trap.

As soon as my sister and our cousin arrived, the intelligence captured them for being part of the demonstration. It was crazy. Still, Wafa couldn't deny it; she had been demonstrating.

They knew where we were living. They knew all our details. They'd been watching us.

My sister and I lived together in an apartment fifteen minutes from Security Square, in the center of Damascus. Many of the detention facilities are there.

The security drove back to our house with my sister, her friend, and my cousin. By this time, it was around 1:00am.

I was awake, waiting for Wafa to come back when they knocked. I opened the door in my pajamas, and standing there with my sister, I saw the security men: four or five of them. They were big, like animals. Not even men, I swear. *Shabiha,* we call them. It means ghosts or shadows. It's the name of the Assad Intelligence.

At the door, they just pushed me aside and barreled into the house. In shock, I immediately started crying. I cried because I knew what it meant for them to be there. I cried because I saw my sister with them.

They started searching the house in a crazy, crazy way. Roughly. Searching in the couches. Tossing everything on the floor. Ransacking everything. This was a student's house, such a small space, and they were trashing it.

Immediately they took our cell phones and disconnected the home telephone so we couldn't communicate with anyone. While they were searching the house they were telling me, "Oh, your sister is a spy because she is a journalist. She works for *Al Jazeera* and she's reporting against the government. Plus, you both go to demonstrations. We saw pictures of you."

We stayed silent.

They continued: "We don't understand why you are against the government, you're a minority." (We do belong to a minority—Ismaili—and in general minorities would be pro-regime in Syria.) "We don't understand, you have everything, you have a privileged life, why would you be against the government, why would you be against your president, the father, the Godfather?"

Wafa and I would not say anything. But I was crying. It was really terrifying. They could be really terrifying.

Finally, I said, "No, wait, no, we love him, we're not against the president. Who said so?"

"Okay," the head *Shabiha* said, "give us the equipment your sister uses to report to *Al Jazeera*."

I said we don't have it. They were looking for something like a satellite phone that they believed she would have used to communicate with *Al Jazeera*. And we literally did not have it, because my sister wasn't working with *Al Jazeera*—she was organizing demonstrations, and only with a small group in Damascus.

Of course they did not listen. "You're coming with us," they ordered.

I begged them to let me change out of my pajamas. They were all men.

"All right," the lead one said. "Go to the other room and change."

In the bedroom there was another phone they did not know about. They didn't see it because the house is very old. I picked up the phone and I called my friend, also living in Damascus. He wasn't home but his mom answered. I said to tell my friend to call my mom and say we got detained. I immediately hung up the phone and disconnected it so she couldn't call back. Then I changed quickly and went back to the other room.

They took us down the stairs and outside to where a van was waiting for us. I couldn't stop crying. Even as they were threatening to beat me up, I kept on sobbing. They didn't want the neighbors to see them taking girls. It still was the early days of the revolution; they tried not to be very public about their extremism and violence. Now it's a different story. They don't care anymore.

We got into the waiting van, and I saw my cousin Amr and the other friend.

"Wait," I said, "you're here, also?" I knew their presence presented a big problem, because that meant the whole group had been captured. Nothing, then, could be denied.

While we were in the van, our cell phones, held by the *Shabiha,* started ringing. They made Wafa answer hers. It was my mom. My friend had managed to reach her to tell her what was going on. The *Shabiha* ordered Wafa to say, "Momma, we're bringing food." By then, it was after 1:30am.

"No, no!" my mom said. "Talk to me!"

The *Shabiha* had a gun pointed at my sister's head while she was speaking, so she repeated, "Momma, we're bringing food," and then hung up on her.

At that moment, my mom understood that we were detained. My dad was also being held. He'd been arrested just about a month before. Now she had the three of us detained. And in different places.

After that the *Shabiha* turned off our phones.

There was another friend they wanted us to trap. They knew he also worked with us. They made my sister call him and say, "Hey, could you meet me now?" He said yes, agreed to a time and place, and when we arrived he was captured with us.

Now five of us in that van.

Somehow, I was silent. I was done with crying and I was done with begging. It was over. You know what's coming for you, and you just can't do anything about it.

We sat handcuffed and blindfolded. They took us to a detention facility in Damascus. I didn't know where we were at first. However, when I stepped out of the van, the blindfold moved a little bit, and so I saw the sign of a familiar hotel. I was able to tell that we were in the Security Square neighborhood, but I had no idea exactly where, nor which security branch they'd taken us to.

This was not a prison—it was a torturing place. It's where they detained political activists or those who were against the government. Not a place for common criminals. They kept detainees here temporarily while they investigated them. Then they would transfer them to a prison. But many people just died here.

Everyone knew about this place. We'd all heard the stories. We heard about it from activists in the 80s who got detained there for thirty years and then were released, finally able to share their stories and write books about it. We'd been fascinated by how bad it was. And now we were there, in that very place.

At the detention facility, they separated us, girls from guys. My sister and I stayed together. As far as I know, we were the only girls in the whole facility. We were lucky enough that we were not raped. After the revolution, that was something that happened almost any time they'd detained a girl. But this was still during the early days. It wasn't yet the accepted way. Still, that didn't mean girls wouldn't be sexually harassed or worse. I think a few factors helped us avoid this fate: one, it was the early days of the revolution—only September 2011 at this point—and two, we were from this small town, and we were from a minority. They didn't want to provoke the whole town back then.

We were marched into an elevator. I don't remember how many floors, or if we were taken down or up. In these facilities, they have six floors that go up and six that go down, deep into the ground. You can never know exactly where you are.

My sister and I were left in a very tiny cell. We couldn't sit. We couldn't do anything. I had nothing on me. I didn't know what time it was.

It was completely dark.

Then we started hearing noises and yelling from guys in other cells who were being held. When they'd heard me crying, they figured out that there were girls in the detention facility.

So what's the big deal if they knew the *Shabiha* detained girls? In our culture it's a very big deal. The guys started protesting that we were detained, so the guards moved us far away from all the guys, and into a new place that had lights. It had nothing else, just the floor and lights. This was where we spent our night.

We were not interrogated. They said they wouldn't do anything until the officer came in the morning. Wafa and I spent the night creating a narrative to say tomorrow during the interrogation. It was crazy; it felt like a movie.

While we were talking, someone knocked on the wall.

"Wafa, can you hear that?" I whispered.

The knocking started again. So we knocked back.

A voice said through the wall, "Sana, Wafa: put your ear on the water pipes and talk to me."

I moved over to the corner, and did as he said. Through the pipes we could hear him better. It was my cousin, Amr, in the cell next to us. I nearly shouted, "Oh my God, Amr, you're here!"

"I can hear you, don't raise your voice, so they don't hear us… Do you know where we are?"

"I saw the sign of the hotel. I think we're in Security Square."

Amr immediately figured out it had to be Branch 215.

He said, "I'm sure they're gonna let you go before us." He knew they didn't have any tangible evidence against me, whereas they had photos of my sister participating in demonstrations. "So," he whispered through the water pipes, "when you get out, tell friends and family and everyone that we're here."

We suggested we make a common narrative. One we could all stick by. So we started talking through the pipes about what we were going to say tomorrow. We agreed to claim that we were not against the government, we only had wanted to protest to see what it was like, because we'd heard about it on TV. We agreed to bring up how we do volunteer work with the Syrian Arab Red Crescent. We figured it might make them think differently of us.

However, it didn't work out. In the morning, they came and took my sister first. It was a tragic moment when they took her.

It had started.

She was gone for a few hours. And I was boiling, boiling, boiling. I didn't know what to do. Then she was brought back into our cell. We were given no time to talk. I didn't know what happened, or what she said, or if it went well. Had they bought our story?

Next, the guards took me. It was my turn to be interrogated.

They knew almost everything about our lives. I didn't need to say anything. They knew where we lived, they knew my daily life, what time I went to school, what time I came back—everything. It did become clear that being detained had nothing to do with my father; this was about my sister's activity in the protests. They were after how much she and I might be working together. But I kept denying everything anyway. The interrogator kept asking, *Who do you work with? Who are the other names? Where do you meet? Where is your dad?*

I lied and told him my dad is in my hometown.

"No," he answered. "You know your dad is detained also."

Foolishly, I thought that the Damascus intelligence branch would not cooperate with the one in Hama where he was being held. But obviously they did.

The officer used all kinds of different words to insult me. No matter what he said, I kept denying and denying. I pretended I was the most superficial girl: *I have nothing to do with this, I just go to school, I have fun, I have a boyfriend, that's all.* I just pretended to be a different person.

Somehow he was convinced by my story. He said, "Okay Sana, I'm going to let you go today."

"Today?" I asked in disbelief. It was the next day after sleeping over there.

"Yes, today. But your sister is not going."

"I won't leave without her."

He became furious. "Do you think we're playing here? What do you mean you won't leave without your sister? We're not *asking* you."

"No, please! Please let her go with me." I started crying. "She's like me; she has done nothing!"

"We have pictures of her protesting. It's not optional."

The guards took me back to the cell, where I had to tell Wafa that they were letting me go. "And," I had to add, "you're staying here."

"That's great news," she declared. She was so brave. "You go and tell mom and our friends what happened. Tell them we're going to be okay."

I thought, *no, you're not going to be okay.* That might have been the hardest moment in my life up to that point. I had to leave her there, knowing what she was facing. It was the worst feeling, not being able to do anything. But, as the intelligence officer had said, it was not optional.

Still, they had to drag me out of the cell.

Before being let out, I was forced to meet with the head of military intelligence, and the man in charge of this facility, Branch 215. His last name was Malas, and he had a reputation in Syria for being fierce.

He talked in a very humiliating, insulting way about me as a girl. "Are you happy now?" he asked. "Now you'll go out, and everyone knows what happens in detentions. Who would believe you? Who would marry you?"

I didn't say a word. I couldn't even look at him. He was like a tiger. Scary. I was nineteen at that time. I'd never experienced something like that before.

"Listen," he warned, "if you ever do this again, you won't ever get released. And if your sister, should we ever let her go, ever does this again and you know about it and you don't tell us, we're going to detain *you*, not detain her."

Finally, he stopped with the direct threats. He said that was enough, and they were going to let me go now.

I asked, "What about my sister?"

"I think we'll keep her for a few more days."

Before you get released, they make you sign an agreement saying that you will never criticize the government, and if you do it again you will be detained.

I signed the paper.

A guard walked me out through the main gate. He gave me back my phone, and I called one of the few friends I had in Damascus.

I could barely speak when he came and picked me up. I wasn't sure where I should go. I phoned my mom. She couldn't believe she was hearing my voice. You can't imagine what it was like for her. She told me to go to my aunt's house, a little bit outside of Damascus in the suburbs. My aunt was the mother of my cousin, Amr, who had been detained with me. When I got there, she was anxious to hear about her son, my sister, and everything else.

Together, we called my mom. I told them what had happened. I didn't have any news about my cousin, but I explained that they were keeping Wafa for a few more days, but we had no idea how long that could really be.

Day after day, we just kept waiting. And waiting.

Five days later, Wafa was released. Meanwhile, my dad also had been released. They both arrived back to our hometown on the same day. It was a complete coincidence; he'd been released in a different town, under different circumstances.

My sister had a hard time. She told us she was beaten up so badly, and that she'd suffered from asthma, and that stomach problems had caused her to go without food to the point that eventually she passed out and they had to get a doctor for her.

My cousin and other friends had it even worse. They were detained for months.

I often tell this story without feeling. It was too emotional. Sometimes I just can't make myself feel it. Recalling the feelings are too tragic. So I prefer not to.

You would think that this experience would stop us from continuing to protest. The *Shabiha* thought it would. I think it did the exact opposite.

After our detention, it was even clearer to us what we were fighting against. We'd lived it, we'd experienced it. Before being detained, we'd only heard about it, read about it. But then when it happened, we just became more determined. And it confirmed that we were definitely willing to die for a free Syria, because we knew how many people were, and still are, going through the same thing we went through, and how many people had suffered much worse.

The experience just makes you realize how bad the regime is, how there isn't any baseline of human rights. There is nothing. There is no respect for you. I swear, animals could be treated better. There is no respect at any level.

So when we got released we got even more involved—especially me. I hadn't been involved as much as the others before this happened. Afterward, I was fearless.

I had nothing to lose anymore.

When the Revolution started, security was definitely raised on all levels, from social media to our daily lives. Where can we walk? Who can we talk to? Who's interacting with us? What's on our phones? Everything.

Our main goal was to maintain a low profile and remain undocumented, unnoticed.

This was one of my problems when later I was seeking political asylum in the US after my dad was detained. They wanted documentation for everything I had done in Syria. Were they kidding me? For three years I'd been trying to keep from having anything documented about my activism. It barely made sense. You're making a case that you can't go back home. They know you can't go back home. And yet they ask you to produce all this documentation.

Although I was more engaged after my detention, the situation was changing. The revolution moved to being an armed one, and therefore demonstrations were fewer than before. Plus, after I'd signed that piece of paper in the detention center, I knew that participating in more demonstrations could mean the end of my life.

Still, we planned and organized—just a lot more carefully.

Each demonstration was different depending on the neighborhood where it happened. For example, in downtown Damascus, you could never have a demonstration longer than two minutes because *Shabiha* were everywhere. They wore civilian clothes, just walking around in the markets. From the activist's perspective, holding demonstrations downtown was like hitting them where it counts, so always we wanted to hold the rallies there. For example, we would organize a demonstration and tell the participants to meet at 7:00pm in the market—the main street in Damascus. One person knew to shout *freedom,* and then we'd all join him, walking and chanting *freedom, freedom, we want change in the government.* And then just as fast as it started it would be over, and we would separate and mingle among ordinary bystanders and people in the streets.

It was hard to meet in person because everyone was being watched. Groups of more than two people would definitely attract attention. Sometimes we tried to meet in person, but we had to meet in different places, so every time we'd change the house. We changed our cell numbers and started buying phones in different names. We would also change our customs; for example, for the girls, sometimes we'd wear veils, sometimes we wouldn't.

Mostly we used Facebook to organize demonstrations. We all had fake profiles, fake names, fake information. I still have my profile from the revolution. We had groups on Facebook that we guarded as important secrets. To join the group, five people who knew you in person had to recommend you to be added to the group.

We had the problem of spies among us in the group; this is how many activists got detained. We tried to take a lot of security measures, but it's crazy—the intelligence is everywhere. Many people who I thought were my friends turned out to be pro-government who were reporting on us.

When we were online we used a lot of Virtual Private Networks, or VPNs, for cyber security. In Syria, the owner of the server is the government. You can't have your own. Even the private companies are owned by the businessman Rami Makhlouf, who is the cousin of Assad. So anything you do online is tracked and censored by the government, period. What we did was use VPNs or other programs to create a wall between us and the server, ensuring that the information didn't go to the server while we stayed connected online.

All the activists had these VPN type programs on our phones and laptops to have a secure online connection. Through the secure connection and the secret groups, we could make plans for demonstrations. And if the VPN wasn't working, you knew not to go online. It wasn't safe. Before the revolution we never knew about this kind of thing.

Many people got detained from these demonstrations. When that happens, you start running. Every time.

I experienced one particularly close call after a demonstration.

After that protest broke up I ran away, like always. A friend of mine was running with me, and together we ran into a nearby clothing store. The *Shabiha* were coming after us.

The owner of the store let me hide in the changing room, but since my friend was a guy, he couldn't come with me. He had to hide in the front part of the store.

I had my phone with me, so I immediately called my sister who'd been with me during the demonstration. She'd been able to hide. I told her, "Wafa, I'm hiding in a store, and they're coming for me, and if you don't hear from me that means they've detained me."

The *Shabiha* arrived. They knew we were there. They asked the shop owner if they could go into the changing room, but the owner protected me. "No, there is a woman wearing a hijab in there, you can't go back there."

I heard them say, "We just need to search, it's not up to you."

I was inside the changing room listening, and I was just dying. They were coming for me.

But then they saw my friend.

He knew he was caught, so he started making noise and protesting against them to make it difficult to detain him.

I stayed crouched, just a few feet away, listening to them beating him up in the store. They had him on the floor, and he was chanting *freedom, people demand regime change*, and all these slogans. The *Shabiha* got distracted and frustrated, and they just wanted to leave. They took him out to one of their big vans waiting in the street.

They detained him and forgot about me. He never gave me away.

I waited there in the changing room for fifteen minutes after they left. Eventually the shop owner told me it was safe to leave. He even gave me a new shirt to change in to so I could walk out into the street and be recognized less easily.

That was what a demonstration in downtown Damascus might look like. Quick, and then they were over. However, in the suburbs of Damascus, in the towns of Douma or Harasta, the citizens were done with the regime early on in the revolution. And the regime gave up on trying to tame them. The demonstrations would last hours. We'd be singing revolutionary songs.

Still, many would get detained after those demonstrations if they came from elsewhere. To get to Douma, you have to take a bus. On the way back there were regime checkpoints. The guards would ask, "Why were you in Douma? If you don't live in Douma, why were you in Douma?" And then they'd take you.

Usually when we documented our demonstrations, we took pictures from the back so we wouldn't show faces. Of course, the *Shabiha* and their sympathizers were everywhere, even some were the citizens of Douma. They would be taking pictures of the demonstrators and documenting it as well, out of which became a common way that people were caught and detained.

You never knew who to trust. You never knew.

We'd say you have a coffin in your hands, meaning you don't know whether this will be your last day or not. It was a way of saying that you are ready for anything for the cause.

I think this is what brought us together. We're fearless, all of us. We all knew what was waiting for us. It was amazing—these moments where people who don't know each other are all together in the same demonstration, breaking down all the barriers.

And I think it was these moments that made the hardship not matter as much. We understood there was something bigger. Even though sometimes our interpretation of freedom differed, (for example, the freedom the religious people are seeking is different from the freedom I am seeking), we all had the same desire for freedom.

It's like the pain collects us together.

TWO

I would admit that in the early days we were so naïve. We thought Assad literally would step down, like what happened in Egypt and Tunisia during the Arab Spring. We believed it in the first few months. But then a few more months would go by, and we'd think, *oh it's coming so soon.* And then a few more months would go by. There were days when it felt certain it was going to happen that morning. But with time we began to see that every month the Syrian situation was changing and was completely unpredictable.

However, I think the first year was the most nonviolent, amazing revolution year. Then we had the Free Syrian army. ISIS was not there yet. They came after I left in 2013. There were other small extremist groups, but mostly it was the Free Syrian Army; and then against them, you had the Assad side, with Iran, Hezbollah, and Russia. We'd believed that the US would keep supporting the Free Syrian Army, while putting pressure on Assad so he would step down. And then eventually, we presumed, the international community would take serious action and just make him step down, and then if he stepped down we would have elections, a transitional phase, and justice. And then Syria would be good again!

I'm saying this is what we believed during that first year.

The opposition went through many phases. They had the national council, the Syrian National Council, then the Syrian coalition. One of the shortfalls of the Syrian revolution is that we've never had a leader. Maybe because we've been under the Assad leadership for fifty years that we now have a reaction against leaders? I don't know. But for us to not have any leader, and to not agree on anything, brought us to this point where you just have millions of groups where everyone wants something different than the other; we're not able to come together and agree on something, or sometimes anything.

In terms of the opposition itself, I don't think I relate myself to them anymore. Until 2013 I would say: Yeah, I am with the opposition; I am with the Syrian Council. But as of now, the Syrian National Coalition is very weak and barely represents itself. I've become more careful now with announcing support to any side in Syria, as all of them have different agendas that I don't necessarily agree with. I am for forming a coalition that represents all the Syrian people, not warlords and donors.

The appearance of ISIS on the ground changed the whole story by increasing international support to the Assad government. In terms of Syria, I feel like ISIS is completely overestimated. It is just the international community, the West, the Assad regime first and foremost, and Russia, casting ISIS as the primary enemy for everyone. By doing that, they think we'll forget about Assad, or at least have to accept him.

This has led to people asking: ISIS or Assad? They say they don't want ISIS, so then, okay, Assad.

Globally, Assad claims he's fighting ISIS—that he's fighting the war on terrorism in Syria. But on the ground it's a different story. At this point, there's rarely been a bullet between Assad and ISIS. Rarely a clash. At the very least, ISIS territories are known by the Assad regime. If it is truly a *war on terrorism,* then all the bombs that the regime and Russia are launching on civilians would be better launched on ISIS nests. However, obviously it is not.

The truth is that Assad is so happy with having ISIS there. He can have Russia's support, legally and proudly. And now all of the international community accepts them, and accepts him, being there. It just gives him what he wants. It justifies the Russian presence in Syria, and supports Assad's propaganda in "defeating terrorism."

It's so frustrating. The game is clear and everyone bought it. Or at least they were forced to buy it. And I think we Syrians are paying the price of all the politics. At the end of the day, none of this would have happened if the Obama administration had insisted on Assad stepping down or if the US had launched a no fly zone over Syria to protect its civilians. But how much does the US want to provoke Russia? And because Russia has the veto power in the UN, every time there was a resolution against Assad, they vetoed the resolution, along with China.

When you see all of this, it makes you feel like the whole international community and the globe is just against us, against the will of the Syrian people.

No one even asks us anymore. Negotiations *about* Syria don't even include Syrians. In a negotiation over a ceasefire in 2016, it was Russia and the US: Lavrov and Kerry. No Syrians. It was going around on social media that the only Syrians that were in Geneva for the talks were the servants and the waiters. So how can you say anyone cares about us?

When I talk with my extended family who still are there, I see how bad it is. When I see it on the news, I know how bad it is. People are drained. Tired. Every day they are living in this horrible situation.

And some people who have been so against the government, the regime, now just want *any* solution that will stop the bombing, that will stop the killing. Anything just to have a quiet day.

Even something like the ceasefire.

And that's the conflict within me. I know what's happening in politics and understand there may have to be some solution that includes Assad. However, at the same time, I wonder if that means we will have lost so many lives for nothing? No. *Sacrificed.* That's a better word, because I don't consider it a loss. We *sacrificed* willingly. We wanted to. But if my dad is killed now, is this now for nothing?

I lost many friends under torture and detainment. Those six million who fled are my people. Was it just for nothing? Do we just give up? Would we be just going back to the same point?

I think every Syrian is going through this conflict internally. Some people will say, no we don't agree on including Assad in a transitional government. For myself, if I had the say, I would advocate to make an agreement that just would stop the killing now.

But it is hard to have hope about a solution at any time soon. Especially, as I said, when you consider that the opposition haven't had a history of being able to agree on anything. And now it's only worse, and worse, and worse. It seems we're going to end up with Assad as part of the solution. And for every Syrian who sacrificed for this revolution and believed in it, that thought hits hardest. It's as though we did everything for nothing.

But at the same time, when I think about it, if this solution is going to stop the killing, then let it be.

A friend who lives in Ghouta in the Damascus countryside, where there's been a lot of clashes with the regime, wrote to me about what it was like the first day of the ceasefire. *This is the first time*, he said, *that I've heard the sounds of the birds in a year. Because there's no bombing or anything.*

THREE

During my years as a teenager, Syria was a fine place to live if you decided to deny everything you heard around you. At the time, many people in Syria were getting detained for twenty years and thirty years for being with the socialist or communist parties or part of other opposition groups. Many were my dad's friends. I was very aware that there were people who were tortured and taken from their families because of their beliefs and the things they said.

Of course, it's not like you thought about human rights or those who got detained every single moment, or even every day. But it was always there; always present.

When the Revolution broke out, it was especially obvious in my town. Even though we're a very small town, we're under regime control. And we have a lot of Alawites and pro-government people. Those who were against the government stuck out. Everyone knew them. You could be easily under the spotlight and watched for having political opinions against the government. And my dad, being a known community leader already, was under watch all the time. Growing up, I learned from my dad that our phone always was monitored. Never say anything on it. The intelligence used to come to my home every once in a while, and ask about my dad, search the house, and then they would leave.

In high school, you must join the Ba'ath Party. It gives you advantages, like helping you get accepted to college. The Party assumes you understand that it's not optional. They give you the paper, you sign it. And then, young teenager, you've joined the Ba'ath Party.

In my high school, they came to ask me and my sister (who's a year older than I am) to sign it.

We did not.

That was a big deal. The high school administrators called my dad into the school. There, they said to him, "You know, your daughters are not signing this. It is not optional."

"Well, I didn't sign it," he replied. "And I won't obligate my daughters to do so either."

They knew my dad would never agree with them.

He's always been like this. An activist, even before the Revolution.

In 2006, he'd been detained for the first time by the Assad regime for his political opinions and his interfaith work in Syria, acting as a mediator between different religious sects. That year a conflict had broken out in my town of Masyaf in the Hama Province. Masyaf is very diverse, with Alawites, Ismailis, Sunnis, Christians. But this diversity was not always going very well. The year 2006 saw some conflicts between Alawites and Ismailis. My dad had intervened and tried to mediate between them.

The regime was not happy about it, because my dad was working as a sort of community leader without cooperation with the regime or the intelligence. So in order to stop him, the regime detained him for around two months.

But going back even before that, he'd been a human rights activist. He was part of the board of founders of the first human rights organization in Syria. It was very low profile. Even before the Revolution, everything you worked on pertaining to human rights or politics in Syria had to be very low profile. You didn't want to be captured, after which they would try to entice dissidents to work for them, in order to buy their silence.

Back then he'd understood the discrimination taking place in Syria, and as I got older I began to see it too.

My family is Ismaili—a minority that is part of the same Shiite lineage as the Alawites, the sect of the Assads. Therefore, the regime side really didn't like the majority Sunnis. So even though I came from a minority, because of Assad's dislike of the Sunnis, I had a lot more benefits than others. If I wanted to go to the government offices to get papers done or something, I'd just show my ID that I'm from that village, where they know what ethnicity or sect belong to that village, and they'd ask no more questions. Later, when I was in school in Damascus, I would meet people from all over. *I'm from this village. I'm from that village.* When they learned that I came from Masyaf, many people in Damascus would know that I'm a minority or assume that I'm Alawite, even though I'm not.

I saw firsthand that my life was easier than others. And I knew that this wasn't right. That's why people were surprised that we were against the government. Because we were privileged in many ways.

Meanwhile, my mom was so resilient and strong. Never selfish. She was not in the streets like me or like my dad, but she was an activist on a different level. She helped those who fled, while also supporting us. Many, but not all, of my mom's side of the family were against the government. But some of them remained in the gray area—they just wanted to survive, wanted to live, and the political issues didn't matter as much, as long as everything was fine for them. The gray people. So of course when the Revolution broke out and we got detained, some people revolted against my mom. *How could you let your daughters protest? This is dangerous, and they could get raped.* All this kind of stuff. My mom and my dad always, always, always answered like this: *Our daughters are not more precious than other daughters.* I know my mother was incredibly worried. But did she ever tell me to stop? Never.

But she paid the price at the end: She lost my dad. Her husband, her friend, her lover.

She's the one who I think about the most.

Now she's had to leave her home and family after fifty years. Until then, she'd never left Syria. Maybe gone to Lebanon once or twice? But now she's had to leave everything behind and start from scratch in a different country. That's so unusual for our culture. And it was so hard for her, this transition, coupled with dealing with my absence; seeing my younger sister (who's sixteen now, but thirteen when they fled) not be able to go to school in three years; and having to see my older sister Wafa work sixteen hours a day, every day, and not be able to continue her education at university, because after her detention they didn't let her go back to school (and where they fled to in Turkey there is no school).

Imagine having to see all of this and having to struggle in a new country with no money, no nothing. And to know nothing about my dad, know nothing about her mom, know nothing.

For many in my generation, I am aware that we're young enough to have opportunities, and eventually we're going to have families. For us, it's another beginning. But for her, it's different. But the surprising thing about her is that she's very resilient. She's doing good stuff in Turkey. She's not sitting around and doing nothing, only being depressed. For example, she's part of a Syrian woman choir. Like all of the women who fled, they have the same background, but with many different, and often worse, stories. And so they decided to come together and sing for peace. They chose traditional songs from Syria, so we don't lose the heritage. They perform now in many places in Turkey.

My mom is also learning Turkish. She's fifty-one, and she's trying. She wants to go do something. And she's the one who still keeps us together. I think without her we easily would have broken. My sisters got really depressed after they fled, and my mom literally fought for them in order to bring them back to life, and to create passion in them again.

Even before all of this happened, we had very tight family relations, but after this, it's become even tighter.

I grew up in a very loving family. Honestly. Not necessarily typical; you might even say a very unique family to our culture. My dad is a very self-built man. His family were farmers, very poor. But my dad was an intellectual. He reads, reads, reads a lot. He made it to college by working at jobs like being a cleaner and trash collecting—anything you could think of to survive and to go to college.

He met my mom while he was doing his undergrad in psychology. My mom was studying physical education at an institute, something small after high school. Around that time, my dad was offered a scholarship to go to France to do a Master's in psychology, but he refused for my mom because he loved her so much.

They had an amazing love story as well. In the 80s, they met on a hike in the mountains of my town. Instantly, they fell in love. However, he was in Damascus, and my mom was at college in Hama, near Masyaf, as well as working and surviving. So they began exchanging letters back. Now we have a huge bag full of letters—love letters, amazing letters. Although I hesitate to say *love letters*—it's more like caring, friendship letters, but ones that also engaged in back and forth discussions regarding their political opinions. When I was a teenager I went through them. I'm glad I got to read them, because the letters still are in Syria, and I don't know if we'll ever get to read them again.

This was not an arranged marriage or anything like that. Culturally, at the time, this was extraordinary. They were in a relationship for two years until my dad proposed. And it was a little bit hard for her family to accept because my mom comes from a wealthy family.

About here, I imagine it starts to sound like the plot of a fairy tale.

For the first six years of their marriage, we were in Damascus. I was so young, but I have images in my head from our life there. We lived in Yarmouk Camp, which is the Palestinian camp in Damascus. In other words, we were living with the Palestinian refugees. It was amazing. An amazing social environment. People were so loving, so caring, and so humble. The house we lived in was very modest. My dad had a bicycle, and I remember he had a store for making keys. There is one year difference between my sister and me, and so we're almost like twins, and I still have an image in my head where my dad placed a basket on the back of the bicycle, and he would have us sitting in the basket, taking us around.

In my head, I see a timeline of him growing up in his business and becoming more successful. About seven years later, in 1997 or 1998, we moved back to Masyaf—my town—and he opened a small clothing shop. In Masyaf, my dad met a businessman who was running a frozen fruits and vegetables business. The man had the facilities, and my dad, a very good manager, had the brain. So he asked my dad if he would like to take over management of the business. This was the point where our life started financially improving. And eventually we became a mostly middle class family. Still, although my dad made sure we had everything we wanted, we were never spoiled.

Three daughters. And no boys. In our culture, *no boys*? Everybody would tell my mom, "Oh, you should have the boy." But for my dad, it was not a problem for him. He never thought about it. Instead, he made sure that we enjoyed every moment together.

We were brought up to be responsible. Every summer my dad would have me work in his business. Not in the office, though. No. He had me go to the factory and work with the people cleaning vegetables and fruits, and then packing them. Even though he figured eventually we'd take over after him in the years to come, at that point he wanted us to be with the people doing hands-on work in there, and experience their experiences.

This was so unusual in my culture. Of course as a teenager, it was frustrating having to do this, but now I look back and realize that it was so valuable.

He also took us to learn karate. "You're girls," he said, "you'll need to protect yourselves." He, himself, was very protective, but not in a sheltering way. He wanted to give us the resources to take care of ourselves in all ways. It was extraordinary, given for our community. My friends envied me for being able to have guys as friends, for doing things like camping and hiking.

Since I've been in the US, I've met many people who don't know what's happening overseas. And yet as children, we were following all of it—all from our small town. It was all because of our parents. Seeing them reading all the time. The activism. Always watching the news and discussing it. My sisters and I knew about all issues in the world. They really made sure that we would be raised as intellectuals.

And in terms of making ethical choices, my parents sent us inward, teaching us to just ask your heart before you act. *How do you feel about it?* I don't think my dad was an atheist, but he also didn't use religion as the rationale for why we should be the way we were. For example, I never grew up hearing Heaven or Hell, such as don't do this or that because you'll go to Hell. In our house, it was more like don't steal, because that is bad, immoral, and unethical.

I still use everything he taught me. It's amazing.

This is not to say that I wasn't rebellious as a teenager, like anyone. But even the way they contained me, it was amazing compared to my friends and other people in our society.

There was so much fear in the culture, but for our family it was the opposite. Our parents wanted to teach us how to survive by listening to our gut feelings and instincts. Still, they always were there for us. We knew they were watching, and if something were to happen, my mom and dad would be there.

In August 2011, after the Revolution started, my dad was detained a second time.

He'd been driving with a group of people to create peaceful conflict resolution in Masyaf and its countryside villages. When the Revolution broke out, immediately the regime started playing on the strings of sectarian and religious sects. My dad was working with a group of Sheikhs and Imams in other villages that he knew. He was trying to create a group that would make sure we didn't fight against each other in our very diverse environment.

At one point in the '80s, a revolution also had broken out in Hama. So because of that history, immediately the regime reacted very violently against people in Hama when they joined the current uprising. Many of them fled to Masyaf, my town, which is the closest town. My dad was helping all those internally displaced people find food and housing. But helping them was a crime because they were considered terrorists. The regime's propaganda machine labels anyone who is against the government as a terrorist.

He was held for almost two months. This time was different. He'd been tortured. When he got released, he wouldn't talk about it. He didn't want us to know such a thing. At the time, all we knew was that he'd been held in a very bad circumstances. That's all he would share with us.

I knew as much about his detentions as he would tell anyone, which wasn't much. He's a man, and he won't talk about it. No way would he tell his daughters that he'd been tortured. But we saw on his body a few signs.

The only person he would talk to about it was my mom. We learned about it later from her.

Instead of talking about his own experiences, he described the circumstances of other detainees. He told us these stories of how old men and other detainees were humiliated by young guys from Assad's forces. They would be put in a cell only a few meters wide. These men, many of them over forty like my father, would be shifting between standing and sitting. They would only let them go to the bathroom once a day, and they counted seconds. If you stayed longer, the guard would beat you up.

They treated them worse than animals. This was not even about torture—this was just the environment of detention.

He also told us about children who were detained. The regime did not discriminate. Young or old. They didn't care.

Those stories were what he thought we should know. They'd touched him the most. But never about his torture. Only what he saw; not what happened to him.

What compels people to support a regime to the point of torturing and killing its own citizens? In Syria, the Assad regime really created the "fear environment" first, and then secondly enlisted marginalized people, mostly coming from Alawites, to be the force behind his plans. In Syria, you would find that the poorest villages in Syria were Alawites. There, Assad would deny them access to education. Then you have teenagers, and they need money, and you tell them they can join the army, and once there, they just get brainwashed. It's just the circumstances in the country that for fifty years created these kind of people. It is the one thing that offers the Alawites some sense of power. And money. Without education.

Yet, not to dismiss this fact, as much as I believe in the Revolution, there are people who believe in Assad. It's very important for us to understand this. Just as supporting Assad's regime doesn't make any sense to me, it doesn't make sense for them that I even believe what I believe. The propaganda and its narrative of the Syrian regime is very compelling and appealing and convincing for an average Middle Eastern person who feels left behind, not educated, and so on. Just as Trump's narrative is appealing for many people here who feel the same way. Assad played on the right strengths: *I'm the regime, I'm the only president who resists against Israel and the US.* Playing on that strength is very important for a Middle Eastern person, especially because of the Israeli/Palestinian conflict.

The regime also has put out the narrative that our demonstrations during the Revolution were supported and sponsored by the US. They say the people like me got money to demonstrate. Assad always makes the case that the US is trying to make Syria the second Iraq. And just the mention of this freaks people out.

And then you add in the sectarian part of it, talking about *do you want these extremists to control over you*, and such things. You even have Sunnis who support Assad very much, and you have Alawites who are against Assad.

It really comes down to your education level, background and family, and how much you can buy narratives and get brainwashed, or not.

But, no, we're not born like this. No one, I think, is born like this.

FOUR

By 2013, I was in my fourth year of college, studying business and marketing in Damascus. For the summer, I applied to be in the Middle East Partnership Initiative (MEPI), a US State Department program on leadership skills and civil engagement to introduce Middle Eastern students to the systems of democracy and civil society in the US. The idea of the MEPI program was that I would come here for two months, and then I must go back to Syria to implement what I learned.

I had the embassy interview in Lebanon. I was accepted and informed that my host university would be Roger Williams University in Bristol, Rhode Island.

I took off from the airport in Lebanon with one suitcase packed with enough clothes for the weeks away. My dad had dropped me off. On the flight over, I already couldn't wait to tell him about all the experiences that I would have.

On July 2nd, I got the message about my father. My sister Face-booked me the basic news. She didn't need to say more. Ten days after my arrival to the US, my dad was detained. Not legally detained. But kidnapped by the Assad intelligence forces in Damascus.

I will never forget how it felt when I unlocked my phone in the classroom and began reading that message. Basically, I just collapsed. Without a doubt, the hardest moment in my life.

Next, I remember sitting in my room for three days straight, just by myself, and crying all the time.

How quickly everything turned. I had just arrived, and was very excited about the program. Over and over during those first days in Bristol, I'd be thinking, *Oh my God, I'm in the US.* Now I became so angry that I was here. I could not understand why it happened while I was in the US. Why was I not home?

I was also so angry that I was not with my mom and sisters. And even harder, I knew nothing about them for a few days because they were being smuggled to Turkey. Immediately after my dad got detained, they'd hid for a few days, made arrangements to leave, and then left with nothing. Only their papers and identifications. It took them around seventeen hours to make it from Masyaf to Mersin in Turkey. They had to be snuck out of the country, because otherwise they'd never have gotten through the regime checkpoints without being detained.

At the same time, across the world, here it was July 4th and the giant Independence Day parade in Bristol was happening. But it was not a celebration for me; I sat in a dorm room in Rhode Island trying to deal with the news of my dad being detained, initially not knowing anything about my mom and sisters. I could see all these details around me, but at the same time I felt so distant from everything.

After five days, I stopped crying. I collected myself, put myself together. I said to myself, *Okay, I'm here. I can't miss classes because I'm here just for a short time. And I was selected among hundreds to come here, and I need to honor that responsibility.*

My dad was very motivational for me. He was so proud of me coming here because it was a great opportunity. So losing it, failing in it, actually would have disappointed him.

Somehow, emotionally, I was able to continue the program. And I continued in a good way. I was not depressed all the time. I mean, when I was by myself I had my moments, but with everyone else I went on as if nothing happened.

Kate Greene, the director of the program at Roger Williams, was so supportive. We would always talk at the end of the day. In fact, all the people who worked with the program in Bristol were very supportive, in an emotional way. And in a practical way, they were trying to facilitate ways for me to talk with my family in Turkey.

But soon a different kind of thought entered my mind as we neared the end of July. When I finish the program August 3rd, where do I go? What do I do?

We'd had these discussions before with my dad, about if he were to get detained. His plan for us was simple: leave. He knew detainment was going to happen eventually, so he wanted us to be safe, and to make sure we had everything we needed. But the first two times he was detained, my mom, my sisters, and I refused to leave. We said, we're okay, nobody knows about us, and it's fine.

But he made us promise that next time we would go. He understood how the regime could pressure the family members of the detainees. So when it happened this final time, because we'd had the discussion before, my family knew they were supposed to flee. Immediately go to Lebanon and then to Turkey (at that time, Turkey was easier to go to). He didn't want us to wait, to see if a detention might only be for two days, a week, or whatever. If he was taken, we go.

In hindsight, that was the right thing to do, because they use women to put pressure on the men. We didn't want to go through this. He wouldn't want us to go through this. So immediately they fled, and had I been there I would have too.

But I was in Rhode Island. And the more I started thinking about it, the more I began to understand. *I can't go back*. I had nothing there anymore. Plus, as my dad had said through all those discussions, it wouldn't be safe.

I started having these conversations with Kate.

What do I want to do?

What am I going to do?

I really felt like I was on my own.

Luckily, Kate started doing this research about what options I had. One day she explained, "You can go back to Turkey, join your family, your mom and sisters, or if you decide to stay here, there's something called asylum." She then went over all the various details.

At the same time, I was in touch with another Syrian friend, Dlshad, an activist with us in Damascus who had fled to the US. He was in DC, the only person I knew in the US outside of the MEPI program.

I still was so confused. Thinking a million thoughts at the same time. I told Dlshad I needed to deactivate all my father's online accounts so the Syrian regime couldn't get access to his activism work. After that, I didn't know what else to do. What else I should do.

"Sana," he advised, "you should stay and apply for asylum."

"I have nothing. How can I stay even here?"

I couldn't even begin to think about how I'm going to survive here, but at the same time I knew if I went to Turkey, there was nothing for me there.

Every choice led to failure.

On the one hand, being here would be helpful eventually, both for my family, and for my future. But on the other hand, being here with nothing seemed just too, too hard.

It seemed impossible to decide.

MEPI was set to end on August 3rd 2013, with a closing program in DC. My time was running out. Would I stay here? Leave? Every option had an unknown.

The night before the closing program, on August 2nd, I was with Kate. I looked at her, and said I'd decided.

She nodded, waiting.

I told her, "I'm going to stay."

"It's your decision," she answered. "It's totally up to you. And remember, whatever happens you do have your return ticket to go back to Lebanon."

With the program finished, everyone left on August 3rd. Dlshad came to see me while I was still in DC. "Okay," I said to him, "where do I go now?"

He'd already talked to a friend. "She's away," he said, "and you can have her room for ten days while we figure out something else."

So I lived in her room in DC for ten days. I knew no one there. No one except for Dlshad.

So like that, I'd made the decision to stay. And here the struggle started again.

During those first ten days in DC, I started realizing a little bit what was going on with my life now. Because I'd been so busy in the program, I'd had no chance to digest or really understand what had happened. But it really started to hit me: the struggle of realizing that I'm here, in this country, by myself, and my family is there in Turkey, and my dad is who knows where.

What's next? I kept thinking.

Where am I going to sleep after these ten days?

I had no money. With the MEPI program, I'd had a scholarship, but when the program was done, it was gone. My family had lost almost everything in Syria, and I just didn't have the access to any extra money.

The struggle of surviving became the hugest thing. And after ten days of doing nothing besides just sitting in the room, I finally saw Dlshad again, and I said, please, let's brainstorm about what I'm going to do next.

He and I start talking with people from back home. We asked if they knew anyone in the US.

Where would I go?

If you're a refugee, and you want to apply for asylum, you need to pay $4000. This is the irony of the American system.

For the couple of weeks in Virginia, I mostly was trying to figure out where my next couch would be. And then another friend of Dlshad's would say, okay, I can have you for a week.

Life went like this for a year and a half. I was just moving literally couch to couch almost every week or two.

That's how I met the most amazing people in my life, and the most supportive people. But it was a huge struggle at the same time.

I had to start thinking about the asylum, to gain a legal status, because my visa had expired. Of course, I didn't have the money.

However, I learned of an organization called Human Rights First that provides asylum seekers with pro bono workers. I talked with them. I told them my story. I said I needed a lawyer but that I had nothing. As you can imagine, there was a huge waiting line. It took two months to just to have the interview with them. Finally, we met, and following a four-hour interview they agreed to accept my case and to find me a lawyer.

That process took another two months. My life again was on hold. I was not able to do anything.

At the same time, I continued moving from one place to another. One of the houses was with an American family in the DC area. I didn't know them; they didn't know me. They said I could live with them and be an au pair for their two children. They were a young couple, and very, very supportive. It was perfect. They gave me a room. And they gave me a family.

At the same time, I was waiting for Human Rights First to find a lawyer, and, eventually when they did, we started meeting to apply for asylum.

During this time, I was able to Skype with my mother and sister in Turkey. Initially, they'd been staying with friends. But my sister, a journalist, found a job, and even though it barely paid anything, it was enough for them to become a little more self-sufficient. They moved to Gaziantep, a Turkish city next to the Syrian border, where a lot of refugees live, where they've been ever since. Their place is very small, about the size of two small offices. But at least it's not a tent. Their circumstance is not so good, but at least they are trying to do something.

We worked together, the lawyer and I, for two months trying to collect evidence of everything.

Yet another struggle.

For the asylum, the US Immigration wanted documentation about my dad's detention. Of course, there was nothing. In Syria, they don't give you a paper and say, we're coming to detain you.

All I knew was what I'd heard.

He'd been kidnapped from the very small apartment that my sister and I shared in Damascus. One huge difference between the first two times he'd been detained and this one was that the neighbors—the whole neighborhood—witnessed what happened. Apparently, it was a disaster, the way they took him. The neighbors told my mom that the government guys came armed. The neighbors heard all these terrible noises before the *Shabiha* took him away.

The description of the house was unbelievable. The *Shabiha* ripped up the couches. Everything scattered on the floor. *Everything.* Everything was broken. Everything gone through. All of our clothes. It was like two bombs fell in that house. A total mess. My mom saw all of the aftermath.

And you just think, if this is the case of the house, then how is my dad?

My mom did not tell me all these details until after a half a year. She didn't want me to know about it at first. Even then, it was hard for her even to talk about it.

And now the US Immigration wants me to give them documentation about it?

My lawyer was very, very good. She and I made the case that it was very dangerous for me to go back to Syria. I was able to get a few documents about my first detention. And a few affidavits from key leaders in the opposition, people who knew my dad. My application for political asylum was granted in April 2014, after only four months. That's super fast!

Between August 2013 and August 2014, I stayed in the DC area, moving from one place to another. I worked in a restaurant for six months. As an au pair. Babysitting. I did Arabic tutoring and translation. Anything just to survive.

Because I was very outgoing, I would never miss an event in DC, specifically ones on Syria or politics. When I'd go there, I'd meet people with similar interests. Many offered to help me out in different ways, and several ended up changing my life. For example, the people from the Institute of International Education, who then offered me a scholarship for an English language course.

The support of people was amazing. But, at the same time, I never felt like I had the time really to realize what had happened to my dad. I never had the time to grieve. On any given day, if I decided to be depressed, that meant I wouldn't get to do my studies, my work, my responsibilities. I couldn't just stop functioning for the day. I also understood that if I decided to really go into it, and just go deep and feel it, it wasn't going to take just a day. Because it was accumulating. It wasn't stopping.

I do feel like the emotional support of each other is the thing that's missing for me and my family. My sisters and my mom share the same experience. But then I think about all the support and love we get from friends and people we meet. Without it, it would have been harder for all of us. Maybe impossible.

Seeking political asylum is a very difficult decision. It means giving up your citizenship. But at the same time, when I started researching it, I learned that eventually I'd have the ability to go back home once I became a US citizen. However, it was hard. I knew that even if the US allowed me, I could not go back as long as Assad was in power. That's the reality. Maybe twenty years from now? When Assad leaves and I have citizenship? Even then it might be difficult, but it's not impossible.

That said, this is me thinking practically. Emotionally, it's a different story. Everything just happened so quickly. I wish they had given me warning, like you're not going back. Or something.

At this point, all I can count on are memories. But there are many things I want, like things from my dad. I want them to be with me. At the same time, my mom says, why do you want to take them out when we're coming back?

This struggle for me, the idea that I'm taking our stuff out of Syria, means I'm giving up. But at the same time, I need something from home. I have nothing from home.

I didn't get to see anyone. I didn't say goodbye to anyone! I didn't say goodbye to the streets. And I didn't say goodbye to my memories there.

Our house in Masyaf is closed; there is no one there. Luckily, it's within my mom's family building, where all her family shares various apartments. So the government can't really take it over. Once, when someone was coming out of Syria, my aunt went to the house and gave them some pictures of us to bring here. Those photos are all I have.

After being granted asylum, I tried to find a legit job in DC. And it was so hard because I didn't have an American bachelor's degree. What I had was an incomplete degree from Syria. That had to be addressed. School was my best way to establishing my future. But I knew that in order to continue my education, I'd need to get a scholarship. So I started looking online, just Googling "scholarships for Syrian students." How random is that?

I came across IIE again. They had a program for Syrian students who lived in the US. You could apply, and then they'd try to match you with universities that offer scholarships for Syrian students. IIE program was the only thing I applied to—the only hope I had.

Every school needed transcripts and my TOEFL score. But for me to get my transcripts from Syria? Not only had I left, but there was a war. On top of that, the TOEFL is very expensive, so many of us can't afford it.

Eventually, IIE matched me with Bard College, and then asked if I would like to continue with this process.

Of course!

Bard was just amazing. Eventually, I was able to get my transcript over the summer, after my friend bribed someone in Syria. (That's how it works.)

I feel so privileged, lucky, and grateful. I know how hard it is to get a scholarship—especially having nothing. Once at Bard, I shifted my studies from business to political science. And they transferred almost two years' worth of my credits from back home.

Honestly, it could easily have ended up so different. I always say that to my mom and my family and everyone. The US is so big, and there are all kinds of people. But it's just amazing. I went through a lot of struggles and hardships, but never with people. I haven't met one bad person here.

Being here, I feel a big, big responsibility. As a Syrian. As a woman. As a Syrian woman. As a daughter and sister. And to the Syrian people and the Revolution.

I'm in a very privileged place, and I get opportunities that I should take advantage of to advocate for what's happening. And so that's what I'm doing now.

When people ask me to talk, I share my perspective, my family's story, the refugee situation. I just talk from my heart. I want people to understand that we're not *six million refugees*: we're Sana, we're Wafa, we're Lamiaa, we're Ali. We have names. And we have a lot of stories.

I will take every advantage I can to talk about it. Recently, I was asked to speak at the UN, and I felt so privileged to have that chance to help people hear about us, and to know that we're not numbers. It's something that is very rewarding. It's a very big responsibility, but for me it gives me the feeling that I'm capable of doing something. Because for the first year here, I had the feeling that I was so incapable of doing anything on behalf of my country. And that was thing that killed me—the feeling that you are not able to do anything, not even anything on behalf of my father except to just count days. Slowly, I realized I had the ability to raise awareness, to tell people about him, to tell people about the other 70,000 detainees, because even if you might not be able to release them, you should know about them.

But sometimes it becomes too much pressure: the feeling that I should be doing great on all levels. What if I decided today I'm just depressed, that I don't feel well? There's no time for this here. While people are supportive, they don't really understand. They want to always see you doing great. And you can't always do great. But at the same time, there is the notion that you are the ambassador of Syrian refugees in the US.

Oh, don't call me this! This is a big, big responsibility.

Then came the 2016 presidential election. It started another nightmare that became a turning point in my life in the US. I ended up in interactions with people who were buying pro-Trump propaganda about Muslims and immigration. It was not violent; it was more of an argument. But it empowered me. So while finally I believed they were convinced by my arguments, showing my example as being counter to the propaganda, they ended by saying, "but you're the exception."

No, no. I don't want to be the exception. *We* are not like this.

Believe me, I am thankful and grateful that over the past year people in the US finally started caring about refugees. However, and I always say this, the crisis started in 2011. But because the refugees were fleeing into the neighboring countries, no one cared. For the US and the West, the crisis started when they moved to Europe.

For those of us directly affected by it, this is so sad. As long as we're in the neighboring countries, dying and in worse conditions than Europe, the West doesn't care. Suddenly you decided to care about us when we made it to Europe?

While this is my frustration, at the same time, I'm glad that at least at some point, people start caring and wanting to know about it, even if it took several years and several thousand lives.

So instead of being *the exception*, I see myself as putting the human face on this tragedy, hoping it will show people that we are not what Fox News says, not what Trump says.

After I was granted political asylum, I had to wait a year to apply for a green card, which finally was granted in June 2015. That meant I could leave the country to go visit my family in Turkey.

It was amazing. It was the first time I'd seen them in two and a half years, since everything had happened. I'd never seen how they lived there. We never even shared the pain. Never had the time to grieve together. Never even had the opportunity to really talk about it.

I was there for a little under a month. It was very controversial for me, as well. On the one hand, it was beyond amazing seeing them, and to be completely overwhelmed by all these good feelings. But there also was the reality of seeing their circumstances—how they were actually doing, and where they were living. Believe me, it always could be worse, and I'm not complaining, after all, they are not in a tent. But being there and seeing the conditions, it was hard to avoid the question: What's next for them?

My sisters were doing stuff there, but it was just very temporary. Mostly, they were just trying to survive all the time. My younger sister had not gone to school in a long time. Imagine you are my mother, seeing your daughter doing nothing, sitting on the couch all day long and no opportunities for school or anything. How frustrated would you be? And my older sister would have preferred to die rather than leave Syria. That was very clear from the beginning of the Revolution. She was not leaving. But then my dad's detention did not leave her with options, not necessarily because of her own safety, but for my mom and younger sister. At first, she told my mom and younger sister to go, and that she would go to the liberated areas and stay with the rebels. However, my mom and my thirteen-year-old sister could never have survived everything alone. So Wafa was obligated, was forced, by the circumstances to flee Syria for Turkey. She literally gave her life for them. And to make things harder, a few months before my dad's detention she'd lost her best friend who was killed by a sniper in the Damascus countryside.

I couldn't stand the idea that my sisters lost their chance to continue their educations; they didn't have the opportunities I've had here. That killed me more than anything.

I came back very frustrated to the US. All I kept thinking about is that there must be something I can do. They are not building anything for the future. Seeing the three of them like that, and me being here and not being able to do anything or help (like not being able to bring them back), was really sad. I mean really sad. And it added a lot of pressure.

What can I do? What can it be? This can't happen. After a lot of talking it out, thinking it out, by the end I realized there was nothing I could do except for what I already was doing. Like raising awareness about it.

We don't know anything about my father. We don't know where he is. We tried bribing people to get information about him. They would take money and lie to us. Everyone gave us something different. We don't have any accurate information or evidence that he's alive. Or not.

What we do know is that when my dad got detained, he was detained with his friend. They always are on the same page on everything. Active together in the same work. So they were detained together at the same time.

In the summer of 2014, a year after the detainment, we learned that his friend had died under torture. They killed him. It turned out he'd actually been killed in the month after the detention, but we didn't know until a year later. And his family only knew because the intelligence came and gave them a paper that said he was dead. But here's the thing: He might not be dead. You never know. There's no body. And I think this is the worst part about it: You never know, you will never know, until you see a body or something.

With my dad, we think that if he was dead, maybe they would have done the same thing that they did with the friend. They would have told us. We haven't heard anything. So we hope he's alive. But at the same time, even if they tell us, we won't know if he's really dead or not. It happened a lot during the Revolution—they would tell you the person is dead, then he shows up a year later. It happened with close friends of ours. For example, one woman's husband was detained, and then a year later, following a family tradition, they made her get married to his brother. And then the husband got out, obviously not dead.

You never know.

And I think the worst part about it is you never know if it's ever over. At least, if he is dead, please let me know so I can grieve.

Quite honestly, I have this idea in my head that he's dead, and I'm trying to adjust to it in my life and deal with it. But still, not knowing anything, I think, is the worst part about it.

Now, I deeply believe that bad things happen for a reason. I was meant to be here because it's good for me. Because eventually, it's going to be good for my family. My mom always reminds me: "You're our hope."

My first year was so hard. I was so angry back then. I had no one. I know my mom is so happy now seeing me doing better after what I went through. But at the same time I sometimes feel guilty at having these opportunities, while my sister and my other friends don't.

That's why now all I do is advocate for bringing more Syrians. I know firsthand the support you get here. It's amazing. And I don't mean from the government. I'm talking about from the people. I wish I could introduce every Syrian to every person I've come to know here.

This is a country where you can make something happen. We didn't have this in Syria. I'm not saying it's easy. The US can be a very hard place, a place where you have to work so hard. But in the end you can get something out of it. At home, we work so hard and something rarely comes of it without a bribe.

It's not easy sharing so many stories and such personal stuff. Being prepared for so much different feedback. Different questions. And always feeling challenged, trying to put you on the spot with questions like, Why is it like this? How do you convince me you're not terrorist?

I do a lot of research to be able to answer any person asking about anything that has to do with the issue. But at the same time, you are aware that people will refuse to see it any differently than with the ideas they came with.

But then I also think that even though people may not change their minds, that doesn't always mean they are close-minded. Often, it is a process. They are working things out. For example, recently I was part of a conference in Texas, and at one point we had this video explaining about the screening process—what you have to go through to come to the US as a refugee. The video explained the process explicitly, and then I talked, followed by a Q&A period. Somebody asked, "How can we make sure terrorists don't make it to the US?" In my head, I was thinking, we just saw this answered in great detail though the video. But as I went through it with her, also sharing my experience and the experiences of others I know, I realized that people sometimes need to hear it from a person, not a video, not a TV or radio talk show. And maybe even two or three times, as part of the process of trying to work it out.

Even though I still have my own struggles in life here, I know how good it is. And though there are days when I feel really guilty for having these privileges, I remember that it is my duty to advocate.

It's really a big responsibility, one I'm so glad to have the ability to do. But one that, at some point, I hope won't need to be done.

The whole three years of the Revolution were the best years in my life. During those the years I felt so valuable. I felt like I was doing something. I felt so fearless, believing in something so deeply. And they are the years when I met the most amazing people in my life. The Revolution introduced me to people that I never would have met in my regular life, from all different backgrounds, from Syria, different cities, different beliefs, different religions. It might sound very idealistic, but it was very fertile.

So when I think about missing friends, it's not about them so much as a person. It's more about that phase in my life. I miss those three years in my life. Sometimes I can't even recall what my life looked like before the Revolution. What did we *used* to talk about? What did we *used* to write on Facebook?

During that period, life was changing. And I think all of us Syrians share the same feeling. We don't remember how our lives looked like before the Revolution. Because what happened during the Revolution literally took over our minds, our memories. But at the same time, every now and then some memories from the past come to mind, and it's like a flashback from my life before us.

When the Revolution started, my dad sometimes would get upset at me because I did not go to demonstrations. He'd say, "There is a demonstration, and you didn't go? You just stayed home?" It was never like he was forcing or anything. Instead he was being a great dad, always making sure we had conversations and discussions about everything, and always making sure we stood behind our principles.

AFTERWORD
RADWAN ZIADEH

On January 27th, 2017, President Donald Trump signed an executive order temporarily barring refugees and citizens from seven Muslim-majority countries, including my home country of Syria, from entry into the United States.

I had been invited to speak at a conference in Istanbul on January 23rd, 2017. I heard about the new travel ban, but my lawyer assured me that the new Executive Order would not affect my case, since I have lived in the US legally since 2007 under a category called Temporary Protected Status, or TPS, which is granted to people who are already in the US and cannot return to their home countries because of conflict or disaster (Syria is included on the list, as are countries like Somalia and Sudan).

I expected that the Trump administration's anticipated Executive Order wouldn't apply retroactively. But on the evening of Friday, January 27th, I received an email from my lawyer asking me to return immediately or risk being unable to.

There was no flight that night from Istanbul to Washington, DC. I told my lawyer that I would have to wait until tomorrow, but that we should read all the details of the new EO and see how it would affect me.

I spent the whole night watching the news, reading the new travel ban, and following stories of people from these seven countries who had been detained at the airports, sent back to their countries of origin, or not allowed to board their flights despite having visas or green cards. I made frantic phone calls to US agencies to check my status and ask for help, but I only heard conflicting advice. The Department of Homeland Security gave an answer different than the one I had it from the State Department: Neither was sure whether my case would be among those barred from entry. I was thinking of my wife and my three kids. What would I say to them?

On Sunday January 29th, I decided to go the airport and take my flight back to the US.

There was chaos at Istanbul airport, since the airlines were not informed about the new travel ban, and they didn't know what the policy was regarding citizens of these seven countries. I was allowed to board a Turkish Airways flight bound for Frankfurt, but I was briefly stopped by German police when I arrived there, and then released after fifty minutes of questions and investigation. Finally, they allowed me to board my flight to Dulles airport, where my attorney was waiting for me, along with a small group of people to receive me and help if needed.

Arriving at a chaotic Dulles International Airport, I was questioned at length for two hours in a way I had not been before in all of my travels for conferences and speaking engagements. For two hours, US Customs and Border Patrol checked my bags and asked me probing questions about my last trip, my contacts, and any people I met in Turkey. And to be sure, they all acted with professionalism, commingled, I noticed, with guilt. They gave me water; they made me feel comfortable.

After two hours, the DHS headquarters finally cleared me. Some officers at Dulles airport even quietly agreed when I mentioned that no terrorist attacks in the US have been perpetrated by refugees in the past five years. One of the officers asked me about my opinion about the travel ban. I said, "I prefer to hold my opinion to myself."

The officer laughed. Then I said: "I feel very bad for you. You're wasting the resources on me rather than focusing on the bad guys, the true threat." The officer said: "I agree. But this is something everyone is still struggling to understand."

For me, I always felt safe in America. I never imagined that my new home could institute a blanket travel ban based on country of origin or religion. This is something dictatorships in the Middle East do, not a government that is seen as a beacon for human rights, democracy, and a refuge for all people who are asking for help.

I said to the officers, and I will repeat it here: This ban is against American values and the America that I know and I love. I've been to all fifty states. I've visited all of the presidential libraries. When Trump talks about the US Constitution, this is something I can recite by heart.

In the America I know, no one can say that the 136 million people affected by this policy are terrorists until proven otherwise. America is alienating all the Muslims who are in the same fight against radical groups. I was only inconvenienced by the first travel ban; if the administration succeeds in instituting another of the same kind, the repercussions could be greater than we imagine.